For Indigenous peoples, the (Residential) School system i to affect Indigenous health an historical trauma. Through the sharing of her late father Art Thompson's court testimonies against the Canadian government and the United Church, Evelyn nurtures a space for recognition, resilience, and healing, to reclaim power through his story and through her story, someone who was deeply affected by the trauma her father carried throughout his life. The telling of these stories is healing – healing for everyone who has faced trauma in their lives.

ɬuutiis Charlotte Coté (Tseshaht/Nuu-chah-nulth), Ph.D.
Professor, University of Washington, American Indian Studies
Editor, Indigenous Confluences Series, University of Washington Press

It is an honour to provide a review of *The Defiant 511*. This is a tragic story about the lived experience of Tsaqwasupp – Arthur Thompson's time at the Alberni Indian Residential School. His daughter Evelyn courageously accepts her father's challenge and gave her father a voice to his experience. Evelyn brilliantly guides this book but center's her father's voice by using "legal documents of the testimony, victim impact statement, pretrial questioning, and rough notes from the victim impact statement" of Art's 1995 and 1999 court cases. The power of this work is Art's voice. For example, "Trembling in fear, embarrassment, belittled, taunted, anxious, and dehumanized were all very real emotions for me that morning." This was his first day at the residential school. But, Art's resilience cannot be overlooked. He states, "you can have my body, but you sure as hell are not going to touch my soul…I was floating above myself lost in moments I wanted to forget." As a child he learned to protect his spirit. As Evelyn states, "Dad, they are listening..your story is still being heard. Thank you for paving a long, hard road for our people. Thank you for starting the hard conversation. Education is key." If you ever wondered what really happened within the walls of those colonial institutions this book will shed light. It is a heart-breaking but must read. Thank you Tsaqwasupp for continuing to guide, direct and educate us – I miss you everyday.

Qwul'sih'yah'maht, Robina Thomas, Ph.D.
Vice-President Indigenous
Etalewtxʷ | ÁTOL ÁUTW | Office of the Vice-President Indigenous
University of Victoria

I remember the day my friend Art Thompson began to tell his story in court; when he arrived at the courthouse, he was wearing a woven cape and a cedar bark head piece. I was so relieved to see him with his cape and cedar bark because I knew it would keep him protected as he shared testimony about his childhood years in Alberni Indian Residential School.

And now, more than 20 years later, I see his exact words in this incredibly important book *The Defiant 511* — the full transcript of Art's testimony as shared by his youngest daughter, Evelyn.

Stories shared by survivors of Indian Residential Schools are heart wrenching to read and to hear, but it is important that these stories are told so as to ensure history is never repeated. Despite the difficult testimony Art shared, *The Defiant 511* offers hope through the thoughtful and insightful words Evelyn shares at the start of each chapter; her words somehow create a feeling of safety amidst the incredibly difficult memories and experiences told by Art.

I can't say enough about the incredible courage both Art and Evelyn shared to prepare this book. Amidst such tragedy and a lifetime of injustice, there is a message of hope and a path to healing through truth telling, and ultimately, a semblance of justice as a result of Art's determination to hold the governments of Canada, the church and named-individuals accountable.

Reconciliation can only be achieved through truth-telling balanced with an acceptance of the responsibility to make things right. I believe that this book creates an important precedent in truth-telling, and as the journey of reconciliation continues, this book will serve as an important reference-point for accountability, and ultimately healing.

Lou-ann Ika'wega Neel
Program Lead, Rogers Indigenous Film Fund, Creative BC
Kwakwaka'wakw Visual Artist

As a non-indigenous person working for an indigenous agency, I have been on a journey of learning truths, of having many of my beliefs challenged and then changed, and of slowly and steadily developing more understanding of the history of First Nations people and communities. I was born and raised in Canada and attended public school and the University here in British Columbia, so my prior knowledge was mainly based on what was taught in the schools, what was portrayed on TV and in the media. I have had the privilege now of working with indigenous families and communities in my role as a resource team leader at an Indigenous Child and Family Service Agency, of having many conversations and hearing many people's experiences, and with each conversation a deeper understanding has steadily emerged.

I want to thank Evelyn for sharing your father's story, and for your words and view as a daughter. *The Defiant 511 of the Alberni Indian Residential School* allowed me, through reading this, to gain a graphic, visceral sense of the reality through the sounds and smells and tastes and physical pain and humiliation and shame. This is a book for those who want to understand. The harsh realities of your father's experiences and life are so important for anyone working with survivor's and their families to know. A lot of us "know" about trauma, but the dark specifics of trauma are often unspoken. *The Defiant 511* has filled in the unspoken for me as a reader and will be with me in the work that I do, filling in the gaps of things that are not spoken, and that were unimaginable. This book invited me, as a non- indigenous person to learn and to understand and it also allowed me to see hope and healing. Thank you for this.

Julia Hunter
Team Leader for huu-uts-tsa-up (Resources)
USMA Nuu-Chah-Nulth Family & Child Services

The *Defiant* 511

of the Alberni Indian Residential School

ART THOMPSON &
EVELYN THOMPSON-GEORGE

◆ FriesenPress

One Printers Way
Altona, MB R0G 0B0
Canada

www.friesenpress.com

Copyright © 2025 Evelyn Thompson-George and Art Thompson
First Edition — 2025

All rights reserved.

No part of this publication may be reproduced in any form, or by any means, electronic or mechanical, including photocopying, recording, or any information browsing, storage, or retrieval system, without permission in writing from FriesenPress.

ISBN
978-1-03-831536-6 (Hardcover)
978-1-03-831535-9 (Paperback)
978-1-03-831537-3 (eBook)

1. BIOGRAPHY & AUTOBIOGRAPHY, CULTURAL, ETHNIC & REGIONAL, INDIGENOUS

Distributed to the trade by The Ingram Book Company

*Dedicated to my Dad, Art Thompson.
We will not let your voice become silent.*

*...to all other survivors of the
Canadian Indian Residential school system*

*...and their families, in which
intergenerational trauma stems*

Table of Contents

Acknowledgements xi
A Daughter's Preface xv
Warning Before the Read xxiii

Chapter One
We hold our family connections with high regard as First Nations people 1
    I would like to give you a little bit of my family history 2

Chapter Two
It was a whole different story when our parents were out of sight 7
    Nanaimo Indian hospital 8
    We were doing okay at this point, more amazed then frightened 10

Chapter Three
As a young boy, I knew what was happening was wrong . . . 15
    This is how we were introduced to the Alberni Indian Residential School . . . 16

Chapter Four
I knew they felt bad about the situation, but they never talked about it 33
    Heading home meant that we were allowed to be with our people 34

Chapter Five

Discipline trickled throughout our routines 43

I was not surrounded by adults that were going to help me. 44

Chapter Six

It was like my body was refusing to keep my soul present. . . .51

Barbara Rothwell 52
Gordon Lavoie. 56
Rudy Brugger 62
Arthur Henry Plint 71

Chapter Seven

"Do you have jurisdiction on an Indian Reserve?" 83

We were in Snuneymuxw 83
'You're not even worth it'. 95

Chapter Eight

I carried those words through some tough times later on . . 105

I caught you in my scope 106
'...You've got anger, you've got rage, that's understandable'. 108

Chapter Nine

I know that a lot of people really don't understand how therapeutic this is for me. 113

Final words in Provincial Court in 1995 114
Final words in Supreme Court in 1999 117

A Daughter's Epilogue 123
About the Authors 131

Acknowledgements

This has been a long journey, and I would like to take the time to thank a few of my supporters through the last few years of my writing journey.

My number one supporters, my Mom Charlene Thompson, my Husband Ernie George IV, and my Sister Kalila George-Wilson. These three have been my pillars throughout the entire experience. They have grounded me and guided me through my troubles. They assured me that I am meant to share my dad's story. They have celebrated my success of finishing major milestones. Thank you for helping keep me together to finish this memoir.

My second round of day one supporters were my sisters, Alisha Charleson, and Carmen Thompson. These sisters of mine have been there by my side most of my life. They are my protectors and role models. They encouraged me and held me up whenever I needed it most. They cheered me on at every milestone.

Pricilla Sabbas-Watts, Mary Schorneck, Shauna Dick-Lawrence, Kelly Edgar, Joni Miller, and Lorraine Taylor: The conversations I held between these strong, beautiful women, helped propel me towards writing this manuscript in the beginning stages. They held me up and made sure I knew the importance of the work I was doing. They helped me understand that it is time to bring out these histories. These ladies provided any push needed to help me finish.

Roger and Sharon Brain have been incredible friends to my dear husband, our 'little' family, and I. They both have helped, encouraged, and loved my family. Roger has given my husband a wholesome relationship. He is kindly referred to in our house as "Uncle Roger" and his support throughout the years has not gone unnoticed. Ernie and I appreciate your friendship, guidance, and love.

Charlie George for helping me complete my publishing dreams.

Robina Thomas, Lou-ann Neel, Charlotte Cote, and Julia Hunter: Thank from the bottom of my heart for being some of the first to read my manuscript before it set off to print. You have honored not only myself, but my dad and the legacy he shared. Thank you for taking the time to read and provide your own testimonials of this manuscript.

Now, two people I have never met, but deeply impacted my ability to write this manuscript, Margaret Atwood (Canadian writer), and NF (American rapper). Margaret Atwood is one of the many that have created a class for 'Masterclass', an online course teaching creative writing. In the 2-minute preview of her class, she not only mentions that the main rule of writing a novel is "hold my attention", but she says, "You become a writer by writing, there is no other way." That sat in my heart. Hearing an accomplished writer say, "Somewhere out there, there are the readers for your book" and it helped me realize that I can do this, that I can write this book. Then there is NF, his music is the only music I listened to for the entirety of writing this manuscript. His song, 'Clouds', helped push me through what felt like dark mornings of writing. Especially the first and last verse. When he released 'Hope', that is when I started finishing the book. It felt like a bow was being tightened, and I had the song to push me to the finish line. Thank you, to 2 complete strangers, that impacted my writing.

Lastly, the amazing team at FriesenPress. Since the first call, and my journey in publishing, it has felt completely kismet that I found this company to publish with. Your faith in my writing and shared joy in helping with such a heavy project has helped me through finishing this project. Thank you for all your kind words, guidance, and help.

A Daughter's Preface

My name is Evelyn Thompson-George. My traditional name is Hakumaatl. My parents are Charlene and Art Thompson. My mother's traditional name is Wiic-sa-wth-iim. My mom comes from the Tseshaht and Hupacasath First Nations, both in Nuu-Chah-Nulth territories, from Vancouver Island. My fathers traditional name is Tsaqwasupp. He also held the names: Cha-chuck-mii-ah (kids name), Thlop-kee-tupp (after his dad's passing, 1975), Pol-kii-num (from Mabel Modeste, 1979), Chiiq-meek (from Francis Charlie, 1988), and Gahnos (from Susan Mitchell, 2001). My father comes from Ditidaht, Quw'utsun, and Snuneymuxw First Nations from Vancouver Island. Ditidaht is within Nuu-Chah-Nulth territories, where both Quw'utsun and Snuneymuxw are in Coast Salish territories. I am the baby of my siblings. There are 10 of us, and not one of us would call each other their "half-sibling".

Art Thompson & Evelyn Thompson-George

I am registered to my husband's band, Tsleil-Waututh First Nation in North Vancouver. Tsleil-Waututh Nation is in Coast Salish territory. I had the honour of being voted into this nation in 2019. My husband's name is Ernest George IV, and his traditional name is Swa'ulqtun. Ernie and I have been together for 16 years. We met when we were 19 and got married in our 20's. We share four beautiful children together, three boys and one girl. From oldest to youngest, Ivan (miʕaatʔis), Ernest V (muuwačʔis), Benjamin (čukn̓a) and Vivian (našukʔisaqs). We are building a life together along the shores of the Burrard Inlet and it's honestly a dream.

In 2003 my father lost his battle against kidney cancer. When we were made aware that he was not going to survive, my father made it known that he wanted us to carry on his legacy of telling his life story. His story being drenched in tragedy from being a former survivor of the Nanaimo Indian hospital and the Alberni Indian Residential School throughout his childhood to adolescence. When my father first started sharing these tragic memories, it was not common information shared at the time. The residential schools of Canada were once a very taboo topic that no one outside of a Canadian sanctioned Indian reserve really understood. For most, the institutions that were being run were known as being catholic boarding schools for Indians and that was that. The legacy those institutions gave our children was not that of education, but deep scars that shame would try and bury. That shame worked for many survivors; it is what kept my father silent for so long.

My parents started dating after ending their own separate dysfunctional relationships. My dad wanted a child with my mother and practically begged to have me. By the time my parents became a couple, my older sister was already 9, almost 10 so my mom wasn't entirely excited to have a newborn all over again. My dad won the battle and they had me about two years later. I am both my parents last child. My father had eight children prior to his marriage with my mom from three separate women. My mom had my older sister from a previous marriage. Both my parents entered their relationship with their own personal demons not knowing or understanding how to deal with their past abuses and trauma, causing them to deal with disagreements in an unhealthy way.

This is one of the reasons I have chosen to write this book and these words. To show my parents strength and resilience. To show there is a positive outcome past the hurt that comes with healing. When my parents got together, my father was a residential school survivor who had not found his voice yet and an emerging artist. My mother grew up with a stepdad who was a residential school survivor and grew up in family violence. She has also been previously married to a residential school survivor who was also deeply broken and traumatized, leaving my mom no choice but to leave this relationship. My mother never attended a residential school, but she was a victim of abuse and bullying at a very early age, causing her to drop out of school in grade eight. When my parents decided to build a life together, they did not have enough possessions to fill a two-bedroom apartment. There were multiple points in my parents' life together where their choices changed our lives. My parents' life experiences let me witness absolute magic, and strength at a young age. They worked their way up from a two-bedroom apartment in the city to a five-bedroom home in the suburbs.

My parents decided to grow together. My mother described their early marriage as nice but challenging. She noticed that my father had quarks that he would not spend a lot of time explaining or would avoid having to explain. Weird things, like we were not allowed to have our hands on the table while we would eat, the dishes were never allowed to pile up, and we would have a rigid set schedule. It never felt like enough to be upset about, so my mom would just deal with the behaviour rather than complaining about it. There would be several times through the year where things would go too far and feelings would be hurt, words would be said, and some form of domestic abuse would be a result of some argument. There was one night where a line had to be drawn and my mother decided enough was enough. She refused to put up with my father's behaviour and demanded he seek out treatment. He was served with an ultimatum, and he refused to feel like he failed at another relationship and lost another family.

A common misconception about a treatment centre is that you are there to resolve your issues with only drugs or alcohol, but really it could be about so much more. When my parents enrolled in Tsow-Tun-Le-lum, they did not realize the effect of the healing that would happen behind their doors. After my father worked the Tsow-Tun-Le-lum program, my mother witnessed the change in her spouse, and she wanted the same clarity. My mother went through the same program the following year. This centre was the first of many different programs my parents would enrol in together. Growth happened with maturity and time. My father's art career was starting to bloom, and my mother returned back to school. Growth was always one of our families' strongest suits, and we all wore it quite well.

After having me, my parents agreed that returning back to school would be the best option for my mother. When I turned three my mother went back to school and completed her GED diploma. After her graduation she would go on to enrol in Camosun College in Victoria. It was my mother's educational growth that propelled my parents in a state of healing. Both paths my parents walked led them towards monumental moments in our life, and those that walked beside us.

I grew up in a home where my father worked full time from home, which provided him the flexibility of being the family man he always wanted to be. My mother was a straight 'A' university student and most of the time I was worried they would be the toughest act to follow. My parents broke their backs to give our family the life they always dreamt of, and I'd like to say that none of us took that for granted. Growing up, I was always surrounded by both sides of my family. Each and everyone of us healing and finding our place in the world. I was loved as a child, by both families. My parents raised me in the city, away from what you would call our traditional lands. At the time, my mom was pursuing her education, and my father had better connections to his art world in the city. I've always been grateful that my parents raised me in the city but gave me the best of our homelands as well.

Both sides of my family are rich in culture. To be honest, I had always imagined and assumed that all First Nations people led the same lives my parents provided for me. We travelled every winter to Potlatches back at 'home' and would attend whatever ceremonies through the year. My father always took care of us culturally in the city too. I grew up learning protocol and dancing by the women in my families; my Grandma Flossy from Ditidaht and my Auntie Pretty (Missbun) from Tseshaht, for me these were the women I would search for. Those women held my attention behind the curtain. When I close my eyes, I can still hear the beat of my dad's elk-hide drum and imagine what it was like to hear his voice while he would sing or chant.

I was raised in what so many of our people would describe as an old school way of thinking, yet they also gave me the proper tools I needed to navigate this new century way of life. My parents taught me how to talk. They taught me that it really doesn't matter how hard a conversation is going to be, you still need to have them. Conversations are sometimes uncomfortable, yet we need to push through that discomfort and power through to have the positive outcomes. Sometimes we struggle internally because of self doubt or anxiety of what others will think about our life experiences. The struggle alone is a large reason why residential school experiences are not talked about, because of the anxiety of someone knowing your childhood trauma; those personal traumatic pains.

My father's life experiences were shared with his family. He talked to his children about what he went through and how it made him the person he was. With healing, he was able to open up and bring to light as to why he had done the things he had done, said the things he would say, or even react the way he reacted. Talking is what helped us understand what happened to our father behind the doors of the Alberni Indian Residential School. From a young age I was taught how this educational institution took away my father's childhood innocence. My father was treated like a caged animal at a young age. These awful experiences left imprints in my father's soul that changed who he could be for at least two decades. Without the proper help to heal, I can not imagine where my father's life could have ended up. Had my father chose to give up, I would not be here today.

My father made the choice to have the hard conversations about his childhood experiences. He decided that he was not going to hold back, and he shared the worst of his experiences. This was all in the hopes to move on and leave those imprisoned times behind. In an effort to mend the broken man he had become; he healed the child within. He was an inspiration to many around him, and many that would come after. There was a point he reached in his own self healing where he was approached with a question, one that would change our lives once again.

'Why don't you take those bastards to court?' The Nuremberg trials were an example of why taking his abusers to court seemed as if it could be a plausible idea. Remaining Nazi leaders and German industrialists, doctors and lawyers were brought to justice by a group of International Allies for their invasions of other Countries and the atrocities against the citizens of World War II. That word, atrocities is a very common word we use today when we speak of the Indian Residential School system in North America. The Nuremberg trails became a very important precedent for dealing with genocide and crimes against humanity.

My father was one of our pioneer warriors in the beginning conversations about our residential school history. He fought to make sure his story was made permanent within our Canadian legal system. He wanted to make sure people knew his truth in a system he was placed in as a child. After all this time since he closed the doors on those court rooms, his legacy of bravery needs to be memorialized. In my opinion, one of the most important points in Father's life story, was that when he decided that he was going to take a stand and go to court for his abuses suffered at the hands of Arthur Henry

Plint, he also went to court in arms with 17 other men. It was men that took one of the first publicly known Residential School abuser to court to hold him accountable for his actions. For myself growing up, this was another taboo subject—abuse towards men. Abuse was frequently happening to women, and it was an open topic of discussion, but for a man, no man would actually put up with any type of abuse. That never made sense to me, not only are men human, but men were boys at one point too. Boys that do not always have the words to say "no", or the strength to stop said abuse. There were boys being raped daily in these institutions. Shame kept that secret for too long. Imagine a life beyond these institution walls and growing into an adult. How would you respond to the growth from an abused boy to an adult in a sexual relationship. For some men, they would further the acts of sexual violence with their spouses by upholding dominance. It was about having full control, and when you feel like you have it, it never seems like it is enough. Some would grow with distorted views on sexuality because of their past, and hardly any sought out help because of the shame that was attached to those forced sexual acts as a child. These men grew up in an age where male rape wasn't a topic of discussion, so they would fall silent for decades. In 1995, being a man and standing in front of court stating that he/they were abused as a child was a strength not everyone can understand.

On May 27th, 2021, there was an announcement made that there had been ground penetrating radar technology on the grounds of the former Kamloops Indian Residential School that found 215 bodies of former students. The local leadership found evidence of unmarked graves on a government mandated school. This proved what we as First Nations people of Canada already knew to be true; or at least I was raised to believe something so horrible was true. It took me about a week to have a proper comment about the earth-shattering news. Children were found in unmarked graves. 215 families sent their children to school, or had their children taken from them, and they never came back.

Giving my father a voice to his experiences again after having lost him to cancer twenty years ago has been a wild ride. I've always known it was an important story to share, I just never realized it would be me putting those words to paper. I knew that his story had to be done right and done in a way he would be proud. I studied and rearranged his legal documents into what you are about to read. This story is not mine to give credit to. I made sure to arrange his memories into a fluid message. This is a collaboration like no other. I refuse for his life's work to go unnoticed because he would have loved to be here to participate and be involved in all of what is going on now following 2021. This story is told in his first-person narrative, as most of these words are his own. With the beginning of each chapter, I start with my own words.

Warning Before the Read

Please understand that the body of words you are about to read are very frank and straightforward, as my father, Arthur Ivan Thompson describes his numerous abuses. My father was one of the first survivors to speak out against the violence laid upon him at a young age, within the walls of a Canadian mandated and legislated Indian residential school.

Historically these schools were created to erase the savage Indian and replace our cultural ways with a more 'civilized European' ways. What really happened was settlers of Canada were uncomfortable with experiences and cultures they didn't understand, so erasing it would be easier than taking the time to understand the differences. One of the last acts of conformity was to take First Nations children and mandate their presence in a fenced abusive institution where they would be held for ten months out of a calendar year and in some cases, children were in the institutions all year round. Many children would walk into these institutions with the understanding they were present for educational teachings but would leave broken and no longer hold the innocence a child deserves.

These children were learning how to simply survive. Children were being abused and tormented daily. Many forms of abuse took place in these institutions. Some of the abuses practiced on the children were nutritional, mental, physical, cultural, emotional, religious, psychological, verbal, sexual, and even exploitation. Survival was conforming to a stranger's standard. These children were enrolled in an institution that would transform 'bad' children into shattered pieces of 'good' children. These children would leave these institutions with low self worth and very unhealthy ways to cope with their trauma.

This composition you are about to read are the legal documents of the testimony, victim impact statement, pretrial questioning, and rough notes for the victim impact statement for my father's court documents of his 1995, and 1999 provincial court and supreme court cases. These are the memories my father spent countless hours recounting to share before a judge. These memories were filled with triggers and had my father crippled in grief as he shared his story. There were times my mother would find my father crying, curled up in a fetal position in bed after having recounted a memory. What you are about to read were some of my father's worst memories of a place he was held captive by the government of Canada. He was forced to attend the Alberni Indian Residential School in Port Alberni with his three siblings. The following memories are what my father told in court to hold the Government of Canada, The United Church of Canada, and his abusers accountable for their part in his horrific upbringing. It was very important to my father to tell his truth, and to make sure his story was told and written within our legal history.

"Many people come to your courts seeking revenge; I come here seeking understanding, I want you to understand how that institution operated. Also, I want you to understand what happened to me in that institution, and the lasting effects of the Alberni Indian Residential School on Arthur Thompson."

The reason why I chose to use my fathers court documents to create a memoir of his experiences at the Alberni Indian Residential School was because I wanted to share what experiences led to his two legal wins in court. My father would be left in tears recounting his memories, even though he knew his experiences were more important to share then be kept secret. My father was taught through his healing that his experiences as a child were not his bags to carry around, but those of the men and women who stole his childhood innocence. Keeping his abuse a secret was another form of torture the staff used on the children. Children were told or threatened, that if they divulged the horrid acts going on in these institutions, there would be a high price to pay in the form of their parents' lives being destroyed; whether it be through death, or financial compassion that they could not afford.

When I was in high school between the years of 2000-2005 the amount of time we spent learning about Canadian First Nations history was dwindled down to a week. This week would consist of information before colonization, what happened when Canada was 'discovered' (which is such a joke when the explorer was really searching for India), a sad attempt in understanding the differences between nations throughout Canada, and maybe a five-minute period of time to explain what the residential schools were in Canada. When I look back at the information my public school was trying to teach us as teenagers, it makes sense why Canadians, or maybe the world, is only now learning what First Nations of North America experienced for generations. Thousands of students were learning outdated information and often misinformation about our First Nations throughout Canada. Updating information in our Canadian Education system is necessary. The narrative needs to change, expand, and evolve to celebrate who we really are as First Nation's of Canada and North America. Our history, and our stories matter.

Our time is now. 2021 opened up Pandora's box for the First Nations people of North America. Non-indigenous people are being forced to be aware of our history because of the 215 souls found on the Kamloops school grounds. The sad truth is Kamloops Indian residential school is only one of 139 schools that stood on Canadian soil. There were more then 350 government run schools in the United States as well. Kamloops started a search for children in the grounds of a former government run institution which would lead to the findings of many unmarked graves of First Nations children throughout North America. These are the days my father fought for, the day where the outside world looking in is finally ready to learn about the way our children were mistreated for generations.

The last Residential School that closed in Canada was in 1996 in Saskatchewan. I was 8 that year. The fear of any of his children, or grandchildren for that matter, having to enter a Residential School was a driving force to close the doors for my Dad. When Prime Minister Stephen Harper apologized for the Government of Canada's involvement in the role of the Indian Residential School system my father had already been passed away for 5 years. The government of Canada apologized 13 years after the first court case in 1995 settled in favor of the plaintiffs. A long-awaited apology. Our culture was never wrong, it was just different of those that were 'in charge' of a country we were found in centuries before the first settlers landed on our shores. It is our time to share our stories of grief, heartache, and sorrow. Those institutions held our people back, but through the ashes of our ancestors we rise like a Phoenix, and we are ready to share our stories. People are finally showing up to listen to understand.

I want my father's horrific stories of abuse and torture to be told because it provides a level of understanding as to what came after leaving that school and how it can cause a ripple effect of intergenerational trauma. Drugs and alcohol led to physical violence. Having been abused in my father's youth, it provided him with the need to be controlling and domineering. All of these negative things that my father carried were held tight because he did not want to talk about the experiences he went through as a child. Many of our people do not talk about their experiences and without proper help and understanding of those experiences, it led to many different negative impacts on many different communities.

Healing is the best way forward. I hope my father's memories can help someone understand their family lineage. I hope that with these written words people can come to an understanding as to why many of our people held onto the clutches of drugs, alcohol, violence, addictions (whether it be gambling or even food addictions), or even more abuse themselves. Much of what you learn in life is learnt through childhood. The way we carry ourselves through life, and the love stamps we hold through life are made when we are children. The children that were mandated by the government of Canada to attend these schools were essentially held back in life. We were given negative life skills that would be passed on for generations.

All it takes is one person to change the narrative. My father believed in the power of his words and his experiences. He refused to give Canada, the crown, and his abusers a pass on their actions. My father won his court cases with the following accounts of what happened to him behind the closed doors of the Alberni Indian Residential School. Please read these words gently. Have someone safe to talk about your feelings with. My father's life experiences are tragic, especially when you recognize the ages he lived through them. If you are reading this for understanding, thank you. If you are reading this for educational purposes, thank you. Know that there are many resources you can connect with to share your grief. There are many ways to further your education about the residential schools of Canada and there long causing effects.

The story you are about to read may trigger unpleasant feelings or thoughts. If you require more support, please contact the National Indian Residential School Crisis line for Survivors, or families of Survivors at 1-866-925-4419, Lamathut crisis line at 1(800)721-0066, Hope for Wellness help line for First Nations, Inuit or Metis at 1-855-242-331, Kuu-Us Aboriginal Support line at 1-800-588-8717, or Northern BC Crisis line 24/7 at 1-888-562-1214, or Northern BC Youth Crisis line at 1-888-564-8336

CHAPTER One

We hold our family connections with high regard as First Nations people

There are three questions you learn to answer when you enter a First Nations family's home on Vancouver Island: Where do you come from? Who are your parents? Who are your grandparents?

These questions are completely normal when you first meet new native families. Most of us start with these mini introductions of our family trees. And every family has that one auntie or uncle that knows all the family trees, they are the one you go to when you think someone's cute because you have to make sure you are not related, as First Nations, we all seem connected, one way or another. You then end up sharing stories of the connection of loved ones, or shared excitement of a newfound connection. Sharing these key pieces of information about yourself help give the person you are sharing with a piece of knowledge of who you are and where you come from.

Sharing family connections and trees happens in many spaces, family gatherings, workspaces, celebrations, potlatches, and many more. It is an introduction to help people understand the cultural *rights they or their family own as well. An insight as to why they may use certain songs, masks, or even screens. Understanding your family history holds power. So, as you can see, knowing where you come from is an important piece of who we are as a core.*

Our people have always believed in teachings being passed down through our elders. These people in our villages are met with high regard, knowing they hold a piece of history that will eventually need to be shared. I think people tend to underestimate the stories some elders have to offer sometimes. I've been able to share many stories with so many different elders in the different paths I've come across. Some are funny, some are serious, some are educational, some help you make different choices. I was taught that we aren't promised time on this earth, and to take in the moments when they come to you. A moment with an elder is something that shouldn't be wasted.

I would like to give you a little bit of my family history

My given english name is Arthur Ivan Thompson. I was born December 10th, 1948. My parents' names were Webster Thompson, and Ida Thompson (Modeste). I was the only one of my siblings to have been born in Whyac. I have two older brothers Charlie Elwood and George Jack. I also have two younger sisters, Sharon Wendy and Iris. I was the middle child of five and the youngest of us three boys.

My Ditidaht name is Tsaqwasupp. This name that I received is from my father's family. It has been in my lineage for many generations. I hold that name with great respect and honour for my family. The other Ditidaht name I have held is Thlop-kee-tupp. My Salish name comes from my mother's side and that name is Pol kee num. The origins of that name come from Snuneymuxw band. Both sides of my family, Boo-Qwilla, my grandfather from Ditidaht First Nation and Sahilton, my grandfather from Cowichan First Nation had respectful chieftain status.

Whyac, my village, was on the Western most end of Nitnat Lake looking out towards the Pacific on Vancouver Island, British Columbia, Canada. This is where I was born. My village was peaceful, and serene. It was isolated, only locals. It was a close-knit village where only 11 different families resided. It was my safe space, and it was home. Our common language we spoke was Ditidaht. Whyac was beautiful. I was surrounded by elders the entire time when I was home. My parents, and paternal grandparents being the two main couples I would be around the most as a youngin'. There was always a sense of security when I was with them. I never questioned their love for me. I remember being held with love at an early age, feeling their devotion for me. All the people in the village were my family. My village was an extension of that security I felt with my immediate family. When I would walk around my village, people would ask me if I was alright. Everyone knew everyone in my village. When I would hop on my father's chair at home, I would admire his view. My dad would sit near a window that would overlook the bay. The water would be rushing in and out, and I would get lost in the sparkle hitting the waves. You could lose time by watching the movement of the water. It was always a fond memory of mine, to be perched up where my father would be.

My mother was trilingual. She spoke both her native tongue of Hul'q'umi'num, from Quw'utsun (Cowichan) and Snuneymuxw (Nanaimo), as well as Ditidaht. My father spoke Ditidaht, as well as both of my paternal grandparents. I was also fortunate enough to have time with my great grandmother from my father's side. I remember her up until around my eleventh birthday, and she passed on. I do not recall how old she was, but she was alive, and I remember being with her in Clo-oose. I remember sitting with her and conversing with her as a child. I remember her having her arms around me as a child, talking to me in our language, and I could understand her. Everyone in my village spoke Ditidaht, I remember that really well.

I would like to give you a little bit of my family history about how we (my siblings and I) were treated as children, where our roots come from, and the type of dignity and respect that my family commands. This is what and who I identify as, as a First Nations man. It gives you a sense with who I am in this world, and who I am amongst my own people. We hold our family connections with high regard as First Nations people.

My father's name is Webster Thompson. He was the oldest son of George Thompson. He had one older sister who passed away before my time, or at least before I could remember. After she had passed, my father was the oldest of his siblings. The name my father carried was, Flutkita. This name was a big, big name in our village. This name had big connections with Kyuqot, our allies. The original Flutkita's bride came from Kyuquot; and because of this connection we received songs from Kyuquot. Many people knew who Flutkita was and knew why he deserved this respect that was shown.

My paternal grandfather's name was George Thompson. The name my grandfather carried was Boo-Qwilla. In my remembrance, Boo-Qwilla was the third chief in Ditidaht. Before colonization, Boo-Qwilla was part of a war between Chiefs. He was a big person in our village. Boo-Qwilla would go out and protect my village and all its territory. My people had a big territory, one of the biggest of this island. Our territory stretched from Ditidaht, which is Jordan River, all the way up to Cape Beale. Right at the entrance of Barkley Sound. It stretched that far North-South on the west coast of the island. It stretched Far East as Lake Cowichan and encompassed almost the whole lake. There were even some allowances for our people to go into the village called Somenos, which was almost downtown Duncan. Our people had big territory. Before colonization that name, Boo-Qwilla, I am sure it sent shivers up people's spines because our people were known to be warriors.

My paternal grandmother's name was Helen Mary Thompson. The name she carried was Tiitaybo. She came from a big, dignified family, the Suckowas. A chieftainship family from Sukowas. Her fathers english name was Jimmy Chester, and he carried the name Tooqbeek. My great grandfather was still alive when I was born. He was the one that gifted me, in a symbolic way. This gift was to be able to do things with my hands, old man Chester, old Tooqbeek. Later, in my life my grandmother would always remind me of those gifts. I turned those gifts into my art.

I come from big people, well respected people. The generations before me were song and tradition keepers. They were people who made songs and gave them away. That was the Chester family, and they are still like that today. Jimmy Chester, Tooqbeek, his wife's English name was Mary Peters. The name she carried was Nuukwa. She was from Pacheedaht. Her close relative was the Pacheedaht chief. Their ancestral roots came from Salabuck, Klalum bay. These were big, big Chiefs, big Queens in my family. My Great grandfather Tookbeek had to wait on the water for Nuukwa. Back then, you did not go ashore to just take this women's hand in marriage; that was unheard of. He waited for her on the water, ceremoniously singing. He sang songs asking for her to come out. That is the kind of respect that her family commanded. You do not just show up to take your bride and leave, there was something you did, there was business to take care of, and all our people respected that.

My mother's name is Ida Thompson. Her maidan name is Modeste. My mother carried two names. From her father's side of the family, the name she was given was Tse ta si'a, which comes from a respected family. This name is a big name amongst the Quw'utsun's to my understanding. Her second name was from Ditidaht, it was Mosstenno. Mosstenno was a big, big women in our village. Hierarchy, queens. My mother came for dignified families. My mother came from royalty as well. As a little boy I noticed this recognition my parents received. That recognition of who they were was absolutely astounding. My siblings and I would walk anywhere with our parents amongst our people. Our people would approach my parents with handshakes of recognition.

My maternal grandfather's English name was Elwood Modeste. The name he carried was Sahilton. The way that I recollect, when I was growing up, he was the third Chief in the village, he came from a long line of hereditary chiefs. I remember walking with him in Cowichan. This was big house territory, and he was a prominent man in this culture. During big house season he would be one of the men teaching the younger generation of the protocols that would drive these ceremonies. Hand in hand with the teaching, he would be consulted in many important cultural matters. There would be this respect given to him every time we would meet someone. They would always shake his hand and acknowledge him by name, Sahilton. He was also a prominent member of the shaker church faith.

My maternal grandmother's name was Mabel Modeste. Her maiden name was Good. The name my grandmother carried was Tthutsimulwut. She came from a big family in Snuneymuxw. Her father was Chief Louis Good and her mother was Sybil Good; maiden name Wyse. Another big house family.

Chieftainships. All of these Chiefs, and I have this same blood that flows through my veins. All of these people that I am interconnected with, they are my relatives. My family, my direct family are these Chiefs that were stood up in Potlatches and were recognized and respected. That is where I come from. I do not have any rights to be a Chief, I have two older brothers. My brother Charlie, he carries the Chieftainship line for my family. I know that he had an unbroken line of children that would be made Chief long before me, but I know in my heart who I am. I have Chieftainship blood from all of these people, from all of these different villages. They are important people. They are dignified and respected people. I come from song keepers, story tellers, canoe builders, carvers, basket weavers, Cowichan knitters, everybody recognizes my family on both sides of this island. Anywhere I travel today, I mention Pol-kee-num, people understand that I have roots in Snuneymuxw. Every time Tsaqwasupp comes up, people know I am from Ditidaht. They know my family lineage and they respect that name.

CHAPTER Two

It was a whole different story when our parents were out of sight

One thing First Nations of Canada, our people, have all felt at one point or another, is the feeling of being different. We are still a minority in a country we are native to. That feeling of being different can range from just searching a room and noticing you may be the only First Nation in that crowd, all the way to feeling excluded because of your race.

Canadian segregation was about First Nations people and colonized Canadian citizens. This feeling of segregation has trickled through generations of our people. Having that feeling of disconnection had taken generations of proud people to push that feeling aside. I am proud to say I have children who are proud of who they are and where they come from. My children proudly wear their grandfather's art on their chests. Each of my boys have long hair and are often found wearing braids. Their confidence of who they are leaves me in awe, and I am forever proud of that sparkle inside of them.

Nanaimo Indian hospital

I remember getting sick at the age of three. The glands in my neck were so swollen that you could hardly see my chin. My parents started to grow worried with my changing appearance and with the urging worry from our village, my parents decided to take me to Nanaimo Indian Hospital to get a proper diagnosis on my condition. The only way out of our village was by freight boat. We had no roads out of our village by Nitnat lake at the time. My parents packed up, and we boarded our freight boat and started our journey to Nanaimo.

I was diagnosed with tuberculosis. I spent the next 2.5 years of my life immobilized in a body cast that was fit from my neck to my knees. The only movement that I was given was with my arms to feed myself. I was left in either in a prone or supine position, with my legs spread open. The body cast was cut so I was able to relieve myself. Relieving myself was always in a bed, so the nursing staff would clean me after each movement.

Life in a body cast in the Nanaimo Indian Hospital was exactly what you would expect. I stayed in bed the whole time and there wasn't much of a view. With what windows I could see out of, the view was only of other parts of the hospital. I spent my days in a room with about 20-25 other children varied in ages. All of these kids were from different nations, so our dialects were not the same. Communication was not something we were able to do, simply because we could not understand each other as we had no common language between us. I was always with someone but was unable to enjoy any company around me.

We were given school studies at the hospital. We would be whooled out of our primary room, to a room where we would be taught. They taught us English; our ABC's, and 123's. Our daily routine always consisted of prayers and singing "God save the Queen." I remember that the kids that were confined to the hospital with me thought it was fun to learn this new language they called English. I remember feeling as if it were some alien language; this was not my mother tongue. I remember thinking this is not what my parents taught me.

The Nanaimo Indian Hospital was where I experienced my first act of sexual violence. Around my fourth birthday I was feeling quite sick. Still in my prone position with my body cast, I was left in our main room while my roommates were taken to our makeshift classroom for our daily schooling. I was left stuck on my stomach, so I decided to rest my eyes. I remember someone with a hairy arm, who was wearing green, shoving something in my mouth. Whatever it was, it filled my entire mouth and it stunk. The only breathing I was able to muster, was through my nose. To this day, I still can not identify what I was gagged with. This person shoved it so hard into my mouth that I could feel it in my throat. My body cast prohibited me from ripping this gross thing out because of my limited arm movement. I was essentially trapped with no where to go, and nobody to save me. I felt my body being yanked down towards the edge of the end of the bed. I was terrified. The next thing I felt, horrified me. Whoever this person was, they started pouring fluid over my rectum. I will never forget what happened next. This person was a man, and after he poured that fluid over my rectum, he penetrated my rectum. As he was penetrating me, it felt like my insides were going to explode. I could not cry, I could not scream, I could not get away. I do not know how long it lasted, but for that small four-year-old boy, it was an eternity. I did not know who this man was, or what his business at the hospital was. The only other thing I could recall was the reeking smell of cleaning fluid. Relief only came when he was done. He walked away without removing his makeshift gag. I will never forget how that felt, and I will never forget what came after.

A nurse finally came along to check on me. Their checks included my midsection as they would clean me from my bodily relief. The nurse removed the gag and in a nonchalant manner said, 'Oh Art, you're bleeding. We'll have to clean that up.' She did not ask me why my mouth was gagged. She did not ask me why my rectum was bleeding. She did not ask me why I could not call her for help. She just cleaned me up as if it were just another day. After being cleaned up, I heard a male voice echo from behind me, he said if I told anyone (about this violent rape), they would kill me. I could not look behind me, and I felt completely helpless.

This is when my distrust started. This is when non-native people started becoming the enemy. The trust was severed between myself and white people. The immediate triggers of hairy arms on men, the foulness of cleaning fluids, those triggers did not leave me as a little boy, and I am still troubled from them to this today. Many years later I asked my family practitioner to assess me for tuberculosis history, and it turns out I have never had tuberculosis. Scaring within the lungs is a sign of previous tuberculosis, and there was none to prove otherwise. That hospital took me under their care with the false pretence of my diagnosis. Another sickening feeling; it was as if I had been their living experiment. It always felt that way, and it was hard to describe why because of how young I was while I was admitted into their care. After having received that confirmation from my family practitioner, it felt like validation of having that feeling of being an experiment for that government run hospital.

We were doing okay at this point, more amazed then frightened

I was about five and a half when I was able to break free of the hospital. As happy I was to be free of this institution, I was travelling to Duncan to be with my family through tough times. My baby sister Iris had passed. In my grandparent's house there was crying, there was grief, and you could feel it. We were meant to be quiet and sit there. My grandparents were apart of the Shaker Church, so I remember a lot of bells. We were surrounded by traditional songs, accompanied by brass hand bells. My brothers and I sat in a room of silence with my aunts and uncles. There was no moving around. When people would move through the house, we as children were always acknowledged. People were shaking our hands and hugging us. These people were showing respect for the loss of our sister, not just our parents, but to us youngsters as well. We had relatives come from Nanaimo, extending all the way down to Esquimalt coming through my grandparents' home. Witnessing the amount of people that moved through my grandparent's home showed me as a young child the type of respect my parents and grandparents were shown in our community. Our guests knew our names as kids, they talked to us and treated us as human beings. I will never forget the amount of respect I was shown as a child from my community members.

I did not get to spend a lot of time out of an institution at an early age. I remember being a young feisty little guy after leaving the hospital. There was this little guy, being broken free from a restrictive body cast, just wanting to run wild and be free. The best part about it all: my family let me. I had no restrictions, and I did not have to follow many rules. I was free. The door was always open at my grandparent's home, and they let me roam. I grew up knowing that I was allowed to eat when I was hungry. I was allowed to have anything I wanted. "There are apples over there. Go check on the fish in the smokehouse and help yourself. Go check on the fruit trees in the back." There was always food around. They never asked me if I wanted to eat, they never had a set time for us to eat. I remember my grandparents had a huge field behind their home, full of fruit trees and peas. In that field was a big machine, a pea viner. This was a huge machine that picked, separated, and sorted the peas. I remember sitting at the end of the machine feeding myself handfuls at a time. You never went hungry in my grandparent's home, and that never changed over the years, even as an adult. I would call ahead to let them know my family and I were coming, and I would tell my grandmother we had already had food before we were going to arrive. Yet, that never mattered, when we walked through the door, my grandmother would offer us tea and baked goods every time.

I only had a month or so before I had to pack up from my grandparent's home in Cowichan, and head to Alberni Indian Residential School with my parents and my brothers. We walked down the gravel road in front of my grandparent's home and walked to a local train platform. A simple roof above a boardwalk to stand in front of train tracks. Nobody was around us. You could look up and down both sides of the track and still see nobody. The train was loud, roaring down the tracks. It stopped, we got on, and that was that.

There was no comfortable place for us to sit, and that was strange to me as a child. It was the 1950s and back then I was still learning about how segregation worked. We were made to sit on boards in the back with the luggage. We were not allowed to be with the other passengers. I found this so strange because white people looked after me in the hospital. There was a lot of caring people there, doctors, nurses. Here on the train, we were not allowed to sit with them, and they did not want to sit with us. White people were over there, and the natives over here. It was a long trip to Port Alberni.

Racial segregation in the 1950s in Canada is what you would expect. A fair example of comparison would be how Black people (or People of Colour) were treated in the United States with racial segregation between White people during the same era. First Nations people were not allowed to do anything white people could. Heck, we were not even able to vote Federally until 1960. Before 1960 if we wanted to vote, we had to relinquish our rights for status. Back then we were called 'Indians,' not First Nations people. The list was long. We were not allowed to use buses, or taxis. We were not allowed to enter restaurants or movie theatres. We were not really allowed to go in a lot of stores back then. My skin tone was lighter than other natives in that time, but I always remember identifying with being an 'Indian' because my parents were 'Indian.' "You, stay out!" No Indians allowed. I remember seeing signs like that. I saw many of these signs hung in the store front windows on my way to the school. Because of these rules, we were made to walk to the school. We got off at the E&N train station, and then walked eight kilometres towards Alberni Indian Residential School.

My family and I made it to the last bend. We were climbing the once long hill up to the steps of the new school I was about to start attending. This building was big, it was intimidating. The building was three stories high, made of red brick. It was nothing I had ever seen before. Buildings were never this big in my village, or from what I saw in Nanaimo. There were these huge fences surrounding the grounds. The fences were tall, with twisted barbwire. They also added an extension to the fence, with additional twisted barbwire; this was to prevent you from jumping over. It meant that we were confined.

I remember walking up these stairs. They were big and wide. We could fit across the stairs. The five of us were able to walk up them together, side by side. My brothers and I were joking about the span of these stairs, as kids do when they see new things. I remember thinking, 'Wow' while walking up them. There was a cement archway above the doorway embedded with the year, 1939. My father told me, 'That's when they built this place.' I thought to myself as a little boy, wow, it has been standing this long? It was 1954! We finally walked through the door, and we were greeted by this kind of burly fat man with grey slicked back hair. He wore glasses and had a business suit on with a tie. He walked towards us, extending his hand out to my father to shake his hand, and then after my mother's hand, while looking down at us. 'How are you doing boys?' We were doing okay at this point, more amazed then frightened. We were looking around the biggest building we had ever been inside.

I remember looking down a long hallway that led into an auditorium with a podium set up front. Cool, what was that for? I looked to my right, and all you could see were doors. Doors all the way down the hall. Nothing but locked, closed doors. I looked to my left, more of the same doors. The halls were painted green, the rooms were green, and the stripe down the middle of the room was green too. The only white you saw was on the roof. My parents were still walking through the formalities of our enrollment to school, and I remember being confused about it all. I knew bits and pieces of English, but not enough to understand what they were talking about. I was just this small five-year-old boy sitting back taking it all in. I remember sitting there wondering, what was going to happen next? This place was just so, big.

I walked back into the principal's office to see what my parents were doing. The desk seemed so big at the time; I could not see over it. What were they doing? I could not see. Signing papers? They were signing papers with a pen. I remember wondering what they were writing. Everything was big in this place. The desk, the halls, the building, the people, they were all big. It was amazing, yet not familiar. For a child, it was all awestruck, like I said, we had never seen something so big before. The principle started talking to us boys. The closest comparison I have to describe how the principle sounded was it was like hearing Ms. Othmar talking to the children in Peanuts. It was so strange because I could not understand all the words he was speaking to us. I could grasp a few words from being taught in the hospital, but that was insignificant with this conversation. I would tell my brothers what little I could understand.

CHAPTER Three

As a young boy, I knew what was happening was wrong

One thing these despicable adults who worked at these institutions were great at was playing Dr. Jekyll and Mr. Hyde. They were seemingly kind and respectful employees, but each of those students knew the truth behind the mask. They would show all these smiling faces while your parents were around, then they would turn around and become something that was totally evil. There would be no amount of preparation for a child to understand the horrors they would have to endure after their parents would leave their sight.

My dad held hope that he would be treated like a human being by the people entrusted with his care and well being. Those feelings dissipated within the first 24 hours of checking in. When the masks of the adults would fall off and their true identities would form. Discipline, Screaming, Orders, Rules, and Boundaries were all learnt quickly. There was this silent fear that would float around the children, and that never lifted.

This is how we were introduced to the Alberni Indian Residential School

After that, all I remember was being whisked away. Someone took me by the hand, and reached out for my brother's hand, then someone else came for my other brother right after. We were being led out of the principle's office. Where we were being led to, we could see our parents. We could see them walking away from the school, walking down the road, without looking back at us. They left us here. They left us. My brother started crying, and I reached out to grab him. I was the youngest and I was consoling my older brothers telling him it was going to be okay and that our parents would come back for us. We stood there holding each other feeling abandoned. You see, my parents leaving me behind, I was used to that. They left me at the hospital for years, so this was not a new feeling for me. Many years later I confronted my mother about that, about why they did not look back and wave goodbye to us. With tears welling up in her eyes, she said it was because they were crying while they walked away. She had to walk away without her three boys. I can not begin to imagine how that must have felt for them to leave us there.

As soon as my parents turned the bend going down the hill, it as if these people turned evil. It was a whole different story when our parents were out of sight. We were abruptly taken up the stairs. They kept yelling at us, 'come on,' and 'get going.' I was the only one out of the three of us that even understood a bit of English, and I remember how silent my brothers were. They did not respond, but it was because they did not know how to. We kept getting yelled at to hurry. At the time it all felt so confusing. All those smiling faces that were greeting us, they were gone.

We were taken into a room, and they demanded for us to remove our clothing. Why? Why would we take our clothes off in front of these people? These strangers. 'Hurry up' smack, 'Right now' smack. This is where we started to learn what compliance meant. Those adults established their guidelines and enforced said guidelines with physical abuse, through hitting us. We started removing our clothes. We will listen, we have to listen, look at how big they are. They keep hitting us, why are they hitting us? We are confused and scared. I could see the fear in my brothers' eyes. I can recognize the fear because I feel the same way. We were scared because our parents left us with strangers, and now they are hitting us and making us take off our clothes. We are no longer safe.

We were removing our clothes because we had to have our bodies inspected upon arrival. How humiliating. Here we are, these little kids, naked in front of a stranger while we are being poked and prodded. It was incredibly degrading having a complete stranger pay close attention to my body. My eyes, ears, nose, penis, and rectum were examined—if that is what you called it. From my understanding, we were not standing in front of a doctor, or a nurse. I was mortified as this white man roughly peeled my foreskin back on my penis and peered at it closely. He then separated my buttocks forcefully apart and without warning, forcefully inserted his finger into my anus. My natural reaction was to jump alarmingly away from this man. I had wondered why this man was playing such close attention to my genitals. Panic was setting in more severely. This was a scary experience as a child.

My oldest brother Charlie was made to sit on a chair after we were done our inspections. Something was coming, we just did not know what. Out come the electric clippers. They were going to cut our hair. With a single stroke, I watched my brother's hair fall to the floor. All of his hair was being cut off of his head. I was a cheeky kid, I thought this was kind of funny. It made me giggle, look at that, his hair is gone. I remember giggling and elbowing my other brother George, teasing him, 'I guess you're next.' Out of irritation I am sure, he elbowed me back. Sure enough, he was the next one to sit on the chair. Even if I was pointing fingers, silently giggling at their hair cuts, I knew my time was coming quick. All of it was gone in a matter of seconds. It did not take much to shave off our hair. It was so intimidating, here we were in this unfamiliar environment not knowing what to expect next from this white man who moments ago was playing our doctor, and now is our barber. I was last, and in a few strokes of those clippers, my hair was gone. There we were, naked and bald.

After our new haircuts we were shamefully herded into a room that had sinks, and showers. I remember wishing I had extra hands to cover my naked body. We had to get in because we were told to. A man brought in a big can in with him. The can functioned like a lawn and garden sprayer, the kind you use to spread fertilizer. As he was pumping the can, without warning he started spraying us down. 'TURN AROUND' he was yelling at us. We would turn, he would keep yelling. It started numbing my lips. I remember the spray hitting my face and stinging my eyes. I could not clinch my eyes fast enough because they were only open for a second. I remember this weird substance burning my nostrils, and my mouth. It also burned my behind. After this thorough spray down, we had to shower. What a relief I thought, maybe it will stop the burning. Then he threw a bar of soap at us and told us to wash up. We did not catch the soap; we were not expecting it. The three of us had to share this bar of soap. The stinging started to subside when I was finally able to wash up.

The tears finally started running down our cheeks. I remember giggling thinking, this is it, this was our demise. We lost our parents, we lost our clothes, we lost our hair. What was happening to us? Why was this happening to us? We just finished getting sprayed. Sprayed all over our face, all over our bodies. What was in that spray anyways? Why did we have to be sprayed? So many unanswered questions for confused little boys. I had never been sprayed before; I had never felt that. Then having soap thrown at my brothers and me, who was that man to throw soap at me? A little boy. Our shower ended, and the same man threw a single towel at us. The supervisor told us, he "didn't want to dirty any more towels" why we had to share. So, there we were, drying off our bodies, taking turns with the towel.

They marched us naked in front of a group of other children that were gathered around to meet these new arrivals. All of their heads were shaven. These kids had clothes on, and we still had no clothes. They were laughing at us, snickering because we were naked. This big white man came up to us and told us to follow him. We were more then willing to run after him, no one wants to be naked and laughed at. He led us to a room that had a Dutch door. Dutch doors are cut horizontally in the middle so the top half of the door can be open, where the bottom half can remain locked. He walked into the room and flung the top part of the door open. I was too small to look inside of the room. He looks at us, leaves and comes back with a prepared speech for us. 'You will get a clean sheet every week. This clean sheet will become your top sheet, and then your old top sheet will become your bottom sheet. You will get a clean set of clothes once a week.' He finished his speech by barking, 'DO I MAKE MYSELF CLEAR?'. He turns while barking at us, "You are 509" towards Charlie, "You are 510" looking at George, then he looks at me and says, "You are 511."

This is how we were identified from then on. My name, Arthur Ivan Thompson, my young boy name, Cha-chuck-mii-ah, these names did not exist here. I am now 511. He says to us, 'Anytime you hear your number, you will come. Do I make myself clear?' Trying to process this all as a young child was overwhelming. In that half second of thought, we were yelled at again. 'DO I MAKE MYSELF CLEAR!?' The screams were so alarming that it made us shake and we quickly became frightened. This was something we were not use to. We were kids, we did not understand right away. My brother made the mistake of answering in our language. The hitting was instant. 'Don't you ever speak this language here again,' smack. He quietly nodded his head. We knew without delay, speaking in our language was forbidden. I knew how to say yes. This was a word I understood. I taught my brothers how to say yes and we very quickly became the yes boys.

After we were allowed to put on our new number labeled clothes, we were given two sheets, a blanket, and a tiny little pillow. 'Follow me,' we followed. I was the youngest of us boys, so I was taken to my dorm first. Dormitory number four. More separation, more segregation. My brothers were older than me, so they were assigned to a different dormitory. When I walked into the dormitory, it was filled with rows of beds. There must have been about, twenty-five to thirty beds in this room. We were all assigned beds. I was brought to my bed, 'This is your bed. This is your bed from now on.'

We had to make our own beds. This little five-year-old had to make his own bed, for the first time. We never had to do that at home. My mother never made me do this, she made my bed for me. I was struggling to get the sheets on the bed. I did not know how. Somebody came along to inspect my bed. I did not know how to do it, yet they demanded it of me. They screamed at me until I got it right. My confusion on this was, my mom made my bed at home, and the nurses changed my bed for me at the hospital, so why did I have to here at school? I struggled through the entire process, pulling the correct corners down, making sure everything lined up properly. I finally passed their inspection. This allowed me time to play outside that afternoon.

I'll never forget that first morning in that place, that first introduction. You do not forget that type of fear you experience as a young child. That type of worry about the unknown, it does not leave you. We were degraded as soon as our parents left our sight. We were children. Separated and left feeling abandoned. I could not speak my language with my brothers, even what little I could still remember. There was comfort in using our language, it was who we were and who we came from, but we were not allowed to use it. I was not allowed to converse with them in that comfort. This is how we were introduced to the Alberni Indian Residential School. I was scared, terrified, abandoned, and lonesome. From that moment on we were not shown affection, not in a loving or caring way. We no longer received hugs, or kisses in solace. We were never cared for the way we were at home with our parents, or in the support of our village. There was no room for pity. Everything was business here, and everything was new. Nothing was ours anymore, we had no personal identity.

After we were assigned our numbers and had made our beds, we were sent outside to play for a little while. What a funny concept in an institution like this. They sent us out to play after frightening us. There was not anything really fun outside from what I recall. There was gravel, grass, and a big barn. Nothing much to be able to actually play with as a child. No swings, no playground equipment, just open field with patches of grass here and there. There was pavement in the front leading up to the school. Fences stood all around the compound. You could see through the fence, but you could not get over it. This furthered the feeling of entrapment. I found my brothers outside that first day we were allowed outside. We walked around the grounds together, searching and looking around our new spaces. We were taught what 'out of bounds' meant. We were told we were not allowed to go outside of the fence, that was a rule, that was out of bounds. Out of bounds were also fenced with invisible lines.

The biggest invisible line that was pointed out was the other side of the compound—the girl's side. Boys could not cross that line, for any reason at all, and vice versa for the girls to go to the boys' side. All the doors to lead to the girls' side of the building were always locked, except for the main hallway. You could always see through to the other side; you just could never cross that invisible line.

By the time we went outside it was early afternoon. There were tons of bald-headed children in the yard. They knew my brothers and I were the new kids. We were different. Our complexion was lighter than the other kids. We did not look like everybody else. The kids, they all seemed different. We could not understand them, their languages seemed funny. All of these kids walking around with fragmented English. We did not know anyone, no one seemed familiar. These children were all strangers. My brothers and I clung to each other that first day. After we explored the new grounds, we just sat and stared. Everything was strange, and different. All of the kids were bald, so it did not matter to us that we were bald too. We all had farmer pants on with khaki shirts and shoes. My shoes were too big for me, a few sizes too big actually. I did not care—everybody was dressed like that.

They laid out the rules right away. Rules of where we could play, what we were allowed to do, when we could do it, how we could do it, who we were allowed to be with, and why we should be doing these things. That was always so strange for me as a child. When we did not follow the rules, we were punished. When we crossed those imaginary boarders, we would be in trouble. Cross those lines, you get strapped. What did that mean? What is a strap? Well, I would eventually find out.

Ding-dong. Ding-dong. There was a big brass bell at the top of the building controlled from a rope. Somebody was pulling the rope causing it to ring. Bong, bong, bong. All of the kids started running. Where were they going? I was so confused. Why were they running? Another kid broke my confusion and told me to 'come on.' So, we followed them. We hustled like the rest of the kids. We did not know what was going on, we just complied.

We were being herded into the building. We ended up in this little room. All of the male students had to line up in that room. The kids organized themselves from smallest in the front, to biggest in the back. My brothers and I, we were the newest boys there. We were there to be introduced. They put us in proper order. Looking at my brother Charlie, 'this is 509', to my brother George, 'this is 510', to me, 'this is 511'. Charlie was older, he got to be the farthest back in our lines. George was a little older than me, he got to be a little father back than me. Myself, I was the youngest, I was right up front because I was the five-year-old. I found this behaviour so strange. Why were we all lined up? Why was everybody so quiet? It was so eerie. It was not done like this at home. Things were just, very different here.

I guess we were going to eat. There was a supervisor shouting a marching chant for us to follow, "Hup, two, three, four, Hup, two, three, four" in military style as we all walked in a single file.

Such a strange set of circumstances going on here as a little boy. It made me wonder why there were so many rules, and invisible lines. Everyone moved as if they were afraid. I was afraid. I was only hours in, so it was all still so unknown. There was a welcome thought for food. I was pretty hungry. We had a long trip from the train station. Walking eight kilometres for a five-year-old boy can work up an appetite. Everything appeared to be very systematic here. Our line up to get our food was also from youngest to oldest. When us little kids started walking through the door towards the dining room, someone was standing on the other side of the door with an oil can. They would be standing there ready to squirt cod liver oil in our mouths. I later found out that Cod liver oil had been used for Vitamin D deficiency. There were always two squirts straight into everybody's mouth. If they missed, you got three. If you did not like it, you got more. The kids did not like you? More squirts. Just foul-tasting stuff to children.

Everyone is just standing behind their chairs. What is going on here? I look around and everyone in this room is behind their chair. No one is sitting. Another set of conditions that never happened at home or the hospital. This was not normal, we'd bring our food to the table and sit. It did not matter who was there first, we would all just join in as we came in. My mother would bring me food. In the hospital people would bring the food to me. They would put it right in front of me to eat. Here, here is different. After lining up, after marching to our chair to stand behind, we sat quietly.

'You shut up, or you are not going to eat!' I remember that being yelled during the first day. You want to make noise at the table where you were meant to be eating? Well then, it's time to get out. There were kids being led out of the room because they were caught giggling, laughing, or talking. There they go, being led out the building. Those kids missed our meal. You were there to eat, not to socialize.

We started our meal with prayer, 'God Save the Queen'. A prayer I had heard before. I knew a little bit of it from the hospital. They didn't have us recite it. All I remembered from the hospital is we would sit after the prayer was done. My brothers and I did not know this prayer, and we couldn't fake that. My brothers, they hadn't heard that prayer that everyone was simultaneously humming. I snuck a peek at them that day, and they were confused. After the prayer was done, we were allowed to sit. The sound of everybody getting into their little chairs, echoed through the room. This was one of the only times you were able to see the girls. They were across the room, across the invisible line that ran down the middle. You were not allowed to cross that line, you were not allowed to look at them, you were not allowed to talk to them. There were so many don'ts. Do not do this, do not do that, don't, don't don't.

Unimaginable as First Nations people, because in my village, we were allowed to talk to anybody we wanted. Adults talked to us as kids; it was universal. When we travelled to my mother's village in Cowichan, people talked to us there too. We were always talked to as children. Here, well here we were not allowed to talk. We had no rights here. We were not allowed to speak to anybody, for any reason at all. Especially your opposite gender. Females were out of the question for the boys. I could not imagine that at my young age. I had a sister. I had aunties. I had a mother. I had grandmothers. I could not image that. Imagine myself not talking to them, not conversing. I talked to the females in my life often. This is where most of my love comes from in my early childhood memories. I received kisses, hugs, everything a child needs through love and affection. 'How are you doing Arthur?' I'm doing great; this was a normal conversation in my village, in my mother's village. People cared about me. Not here at this place. I did not get that here from nobody. None of these white people talked to me like they cared about me. When they talked to me, it was an order. '511, you sit down. 511, you get your sheets 511, do you want your food? Shut up, 511. Get over here. 511, go over there. 511, you do this. 511, you do that.' It was always more of the same. You could never catch a break at this place, not even at dinner. 'You want your meal 511, you shut up'. I would shut up. I would comply.

We would have older kids at the end of our rows, the monitors. These big kids called monitors were the ones that would serve out our food. This big plate would be put on the table and the monitors would have us all pass down our plates for our meal. One slop, two slops, one slop, two slops. By the time my plate made it back to me, I was bewildered looking at what I had lying in front of me. I had never seen this type of food before. What were they trying to feed me? I just could not identify with it. At home, I understood what fish, mussels, crab, halibut, and deer meat were. This, this I could not understand. My mother never made me anything that looked like this. I finally asked the guy next to me, 'what is this?' He said it was macaroni. I was only five, so maybe this was a different kind that I had never tried before. I picked up my head from my confusion only to see that we were being given milk, or what looked like milk. Here is our drink to go with our meal. Here is a piece of bread, but no butter, and no forks. We had to eat this meal with spoons. Back then I thought that was so strange because I was given forks at home. Oh well, just grab a spoonful of this macaroni and we will see what it is like.

I have got to say, those kids that left were probably the luckiest bunch. My first experience of a meal there was disgusting. I put one mouthful in my mouth, and it had to have been the ugliest tasting stuff. I can still remember that repulsive taste in my mouth. It did not taste like macaroni, or cheese for that matter. It tasted like something that was moldy. It smelt foul, something you would fight back to swallow. I remember finding my brother George in the crowd and noticing the same struggle while he was trying to eat his own food. I decided to not eat it, and I pushed it away. Almost instantly those other children around me replied to my actions in shock, saying 'you don't want that?' There was sheer excitement from the child across from me when I replied with my no. They quickly scooped up my food, while I settled with my piece of bread. I knew what that was at least, and I figured, they cannot really fool around with bread. I decided I would try the milk. Taking a sip, it quickly became another thing I could not recognize. When I was a kid, milk never agreed with me. My stomach would knot up, and it would make it so my body would suffer trying to have a bowel movement. The staff at the hospital recognized my symptoms and stopped giving me milk, yet here it was sitting in front of me at this school. You had two choices, you drink it because you are not going to get anything else, or you go without. That day, I pushed the milk aside and went without. Another happy neighbour took my milk to finish quickly.

So, in essence, I suppose I missed my first meal because I did not like the food. Back then I was still hopeful, still so oblivious to the set of standards that were going to take over my life. I figured that a piece of bread was good enough to tie me over for a little while. I thought it would be like at home, where you were allowed to eat anytime you were hungry. We always had all these snacks at our disposal as children at home. At any given time, we would have cookies, or fruit. Snacks were always around as kids. Well, that was not the case here. We were never allowed to just help ourselves to food. You learnt quickly that food was scheduled and monitored. Getting anything extra did not happen here. I was hungry by the time I went to bed that night. All I could do at the time was drink water out of the tap. That is all I could find to help try and fill me up. It became very clear why those children were so excited to finish up the meal I rejected earlier—they were starving.

Ding-dong, ding-dong. The bell starts ringing again. All of these bald-headed kids running towards the building to line up. All these brown little faces running in unison. Every time you heard that bell ringing, people ran. It was like a stampede towards the door. Once everyone is lined up, we get ushered into our proper rooms. It is nighttime, and we are about to go to bed. When we make it to our rooms, we get our assigned pyjamas. Everything we had, had our numbers attached to it. 511 was plastered all over my clothes. 511 was on my shirts. 511 was on my pillowcase. 511 was even on my bed sheets. Everywhere around me, around what little personal space I was given, was 511. It was on my shoes. 511 on my socks. Just everywhere I looked. It became really clear to me that that is who I was. There was 511 standing beside his bed. As a little boy, this is how I started identifying with numbers.

Everyone has numbers. Look at all the numbers. All around the whole dorm was an assortment of numbers. Then the yelling starts again. 'PUT ON YOUR PYJAMAS!' Everybody starts to comply, putting on their pyjamas. Everyone is systematically standing at the foot of their bed. This was a rule, before you get to go to bed you stand there to bow your head and say a prayer. This is the prayer that we make to God. The supervisory staff enforced that rule and made sure we obliged. We had to say this prayer as kids, and that first night, you could tell it was rehearsed. No one was off key; everyone knew this prayer but me. The new kids fell silent until they were able to effectively follow along.

In a very orderly fashion, after prayers were complete everybody would turn their sheets down and get into bed from the right-hand side. You got into bed with your right hand, followed by your right leg and then got fully into bed. Everyone had to do it this way. Everything, everything down to how you got into bed was systemic. You got in trouble for the smallest things in this institution. You were not allowed to jump on your bed. No fun was allowed to happen. Everybody was in bed on their backs. Lights went out, and you were surrounded by the still and dark of the night.

That first night there was traumatic and not easily forgotten. As soon as the lights went out, you could hear the kids sniffling and crying. Crying for their parents, and I am sure out of loneliness and fear. Other kids would call out in trying to quiet the other children, but they did not care, they kept crying anyway. Shhhhh, we are going to get in trouble. Then you hear the yelling, 'Shut up and quit crying like babies and get to sleep!!!'. We were babies. For me, this was almost routine. In the hospital we had the same type of schedule, prayers and lights out. I knew what this was about already. Trying to sleep while hearing other children calling out for their parents was hard. If anyone were out right crying, lights would be flipped on, and we would be yelled at again. They would swear at us, and we would not understand. I remember lying there asking my neighbour, what is hell? Or goddamn? And his answer was short and brief, 'I think it's swearing, shhh, be quiet.' Okay, I do not want to be caught talking because we will get in trouble. I thought to myself, okay, go to sleep. You heard sniffling all night.

Ding-dong, ding-dong. There is goes again. The bell is what wakes us up in the morning. There was nothing that could prepare me for what was coming next in this hell hole. There was no daylight outside, yet we were being woken up to start our day. On goes the lights suddenly accompanied by someone saying, 'Rise and shine.' All of us kids woken in a fright, so we jump out of our beds. Everyone is lining up at the end of their beds, peeling back their bedding. This is when our beds were to be inspected for bed wetter's.

Now, just a gentle reminder, for myself personally, my body was conditioned to not move through the night because of the body cast I was trapped in at my stay at the hospital. I was made to relieve myself on either my back, or on my stomach. I was unable to pick my own body up to head to any bathroom. The staff at the hospital would clean my body after each movement, and it was not made into a negative experience then because it was understandable being in a body cast. Here in this institution, it was made clear that this behaviour was not to be tolerated.

Once all of the bedding was pulled back and we were in our proper position at the end of our beds, the inspections started. My bed was wet. All of the kids that had wet beds were being singled out. Walking down the line, 'You, line up. 511—line up. 409—line up, 506—line up.' It was never personal; we never were called by our own names. 'At the door.' There we were the line up of bed wetter's waiting to see our supervisor at their office. I did not understand what was going on at the time. I was confused, looking and waiting to see why we were in this line.

There we were, lined up outside of the dorm room waiting for our supervisor. Mr. Floyd was there waiting for us boys. He lined us all up in a row. There must have been about 10 of us boys, not knowing what was going on. Mr. Floyd goes into his office and comes out with something in his hands. I recognize what he has, finally, something familiar. He has got something that is beaded. It looks like it is peyote stitched bead work. As that young native boy I thought, cool he has something beaded. That enthusiasm for seeing something familiar turned to absolute horror very quickly.

The first little boy set in our line was told to stick out his hand. This boy reaches out his hand, and with all of Mr. Floyd's might, he drove that leather strap down and struck the boy's hand. The sheer pain cripples this little boy and he fell to his knees in pain. With absolutely no remorse, Mr. Floyd proceeds to tell this boy that he has to stick out his other hand. 'That's what you get for wetting your bed. Get back in there and take your sheets off. Get cleaned up!' You could see the horror in all of our eyes, the boys knew what was coming next for us. Our turn was coming. The fear is setting in.

I remember thinking, 'Holy Christ, I'm going to be next!' In the hospital, we learnt about Christ. They were teaching us about prayers, and how we were meant to pray to Christ. This Christ they taught us to pray to was supposed to help you, but he did not come help me this time. All of these kids, they would go running back towards their beds to strip their sheets. It comes down to one more boy in front of me. I am starting to feel anxious and antsy. All of these boys would running away screaming. It was hard not to feel the pain in their screams when they were being hit. They would all drop to their knees with their hands shivering. Each hand being kissed by this leather strap, and screams would always follow. I called out for God that morning. Today I needed that saviour. I wanted to feel safe. I wanted someone to help me feel safe. My turn was next, and God was not saving me today.

It came to my turn, 'Stick out your hand.' I lowered my head and reluctantly stuck out my hand. Mr. Floyd swung his arm up in the air and thrashed down on my extended arm with all of his adult force. That first blow to my skin, I will never forget that moment. I was paralyzed beyond comprehension. It felt as if my hand had just disappeared. The strike my hand with his beaded leather strap was so hard, it felt as if my arm had ripped off my body. It felt dead.

Overwhelmed with fear and pain, I began to wet myself. I was scared beyond measure, and I was still on my knees when he landed his next hit. The severe pain had my body trembling uncontrollably and with that second blow, I had a bowel movement. At the sight of my excrement falling out of my pyjamas it lit this wanton fury with my supervisor and he began hitting me with that strap all over my body. He was angry. After he was done beating me with his strap, he turned around and took me by the neck. He pushed me down to the floor where my excrement was and said, 'Pick this damn thing up and put it in the fucking toilet.' I could not feel my hands and there I was, picking it up with my bare hands. My hands were numb, and I was running towards the toilet to flush it. It did not end there, he followed me the entire way. I could not even feel the handle and here he was hitting my back. My hands were trembling furiously, but I was not allowed to wash my hands, he would not let me.

I was chased back to the dorm so I could remove my soiled bedding. When I got back to the room all of the kids that wet their bed had their soiled bedding removed and piled in one pile. The pile was then tied up together and Mr. Floyd looks at me and says, '511, you bring it down to the laundry.' To add to my physical pain, I was about to be humiliated by dragging this heavy soiled laundry down the stairs, through the dining room, and towards the laundry room.

There were girls working in the dining room that morning. They knew what was up, they knew I was a bed wetter. This is when I learnt exactly what taunting meant. I was dragging this makeshift bagged dirty laundry, the same size as myself, through the room while these young girls were yelling, 'Bed wetter, bed wetter', followed by their giggles. I was ashamed. I just wanted to be done with this task. I finally found the laundry and I dumped off the soiled laundry that was my size in weight in comparison. I ran through the dining hall, and up the stairs, still in tears.

When I reached the top of the stairs, I saw my brother Charlie. As I was trying to stifle my tears away, my brother made an attempt in comforting me from afar by whispering, 'it's okay,' in our language.

Seeing me in tears, he made the quick sacrifice in trying to comfort me, because if he were caught using our language he would be in trouble. I understood what he meant, but it was not okay. I was not okay. As a young boy, I knew what was happening was wrong. I should not be made embarrassed or belittled for my bed wetting. After my seconds of salvation of having seen my brother, I ran back to my dorm. I knew then as a young boy that I was succumbing to the supervisiors power and control. I knew at that young age that there was something dreadfully wrong with this place.

When I got back to my dorm the assaults continued. My supervisor began to tear off my wet pyjamas and forced me into the showers. The supervisor grabbed a floor scrub brush, the kind with the long, rough bristles made for industrial cleaning. This man started scrubbing my body with this floor brush designed for filthy floors. The body areas he concentrated on were my penis and anal areas. He scrubbed my body so hard that if felt as if my skin was peeling back with every stroke he made. After my shower, I dried off, got dressed, and made my bed. I was ordered to miss my breakfast that morning. Fine, I do not care, just keep me away from that monster. I remember thinking, my mother would understand why I wet the bed. The nurses at the hospital would not punish me for this either. I was conditioned for three years in a bloody hospital to pee myself in bed, to crap myself in bed, with a full body cast. I did not know any better. After I made my bed, they made me stand at attention at the end of my bed while all of the other kids scurred out of the room to go downstairs to eat breakfast. Ding-dong, ding-dong. There go the bells again, breakfast time.

After this first morning there I made a habit of waking up early in the morning. From my first day to three years down the road, wetting the bed was my ongoing problem. I was up early to try and hide the fact that I was wetting the bed. Every time I wet the bed I would get strapped. Every. Single. Time. The bed wetters would receive their strap and then miss breakfast. Ten months it happened like this. I would go home and wet the bed, yet nobody straps me, nobody hits me, I am not yelled at. My mother would gather my sheets, wash them, hang them to dry outside on the laundry line. Once they were dry my mother would then bring them back inside and make my bed. 'It's okay son.' I am home, it is okay, it is the only time it is okay.

Never before in my five years did I ever get that kind of treatment for bed wetting. No one ever hit me so hard that I was unable to feel my hands. Nobody in my village ever hurt me in that way. It was only my first 24 hours in this place, and I had already been hit with such severity that I could not even feel my damn little hands. To top it off, they made me miss my breakfast. I was made to feel like such a bad little boy. You wet your bed, you crapped your pants, now you miss your breakfast. Trembling in fear, embarrassment, belittled, taunted, anxious, and dehumanized were all very real emotions for me that morning. I had never wanted my parents more. I wanted God to save me. I wanted someone to rescue me.

CHAPTER *Four*

I knew they felt bad about the situation, but they never talked about it

Summers were my dads only safe space. The only time he felt genuine love and caring from trusted adults. This was the only time he could truly be himself. To not live in fear. I'd be curious to know how long it took those children to calm their nervous system of that fear, only to go back so soon. Remembering they didn't have to walk on their tippy toes for everything.

I'd imagine, not every child had a safe space to go home to because of intergenerational trauma, as these schools effected up to 3 generations in families. Each family would grow with their own triggers, traumas, and abuses to heal or escape from. I am grateful my Dad had caring grandparents to visit, and a loving community. They had a level of understanding of his experiences because they also attended their own residential schools. Our family was a family that had 3 generations attend these schools.

Heading home meant that we were allowed to be with our people

I remember the only time I was lucky enough to have a break from these institution walls was during our summer months. July and August were our only months of salvation. Not all of the kids were fortunate enough to have parents that could afford to have them come home for that stretch of time. The rules were always made clear, we were to return back to school in September, or consequences would happen not only to us kids, but my parents as well. We were always brought back.

During those summer months, we were genuinely loved. We felt it, we understood we were loved. Being home in Whyac, we were safe. This beautiful place among our Ditidaht people. There was always an abundance of everything we were missing at school. We were cared for, we were trusted for tasks, we were allowed to chat with everyone. It felt like we were released from the invisible ball and chain we were already so use to dragging around. When I was home, in my village, I would be taught many ways on survival. Gathering food was always one of those lessons I would be taught. I would be taught how to hunt a variety of animals as well. We would hunt deer with guns and bring it home for food. We knew to gather seafood like mussels and clams. We were taught how to crab. We knew the differences between halibut and salmon.

Heading home meant that we were allowed to be with our people. Hanging out with my grandmother, my father's mother, was always on the top of my list. I remember her and I taking a ride down to the lake, and as we were going down you could see crabs all along the water. Hundreds of them, all along the shoreline. My grandmother would scoop one up, and then she would call on my grandfather to bring more. She would gently say, 'Bring it over to Arthur, we'll show him, open it up after it's cooked.' We would wait for the crabs to turn bright red, and then start peeling the shell away. My grandmother would peel back the gills and then say, 'You eat that son, you'll stop wetting the bed.' She was giving me Teachings as a young boy. Showing me in a Traditional Way, how to help with my obstacles I was faced with away from home. It did not work right away, but she kept making that effort to help me every time I had a chance to be with her. She would spend time with me, reinforcing the idea that this was actually going to work. That there would be a day where I would stop wetting my bed. It was my grandmother who was giving me support to help me solve this problem. I told my grandparents how when I would wet my bed at school, they would hit my hands. I knew I was safe with them. I could trust they would show me empathy. They would hold me. It made them feel awful to know that this was going on. I know they felt bad about the situation, but they never talked about it.

I used to go out of bounds to get fruit when we were at school. I would raid the vegetable garden where they would grow potatoes. I would go cook the potatoes to eat to supplement my meals. We used to cook them in the incinerator where they burned all kinds of garbage. I remember there were times where the incinerator would be disgusting. You'd even be able to find feminine napkins inside. We did not care. We would leave them inside to cook and just eat the insides. Almost always you would see somebody taking those peelings too. I would take them off because I would not want to eat the part that was touching the garbage, but someone would always scoop them up to eat, burnt or not. I would be caught getting apples and berries as well. There was even a time that I would steal chickens from one of the members of the Tseshaht tribe as well.

From my father's chair view at home, I would also see fisherman out in their canoes. Fisherman fishing for salmon and halibut; whatever may have been in season at the time. There would be people gathering seafood, whether it be in their canoe or walking the shoreline. Our seafood always consisted of mussels, abalone, hyishtoop, and octopus. When resources were gathered, they were always shared. The seafood and wood would be distributed. Our smokehouses would be full of fish, and that too would be handed out to everyone. We would also prepare sun dried fish whether it be halibut, or cod. There was always an abundance of fish around us. We could fish for crabs whenever we wanted. There were times where someone would cook crabs in a big pot that was left on the beach for everyone to eat. In our village, no one went without. When someone was in need, we would all help. I remember in Clo-oose, people fished for smelts in the summer; that was always a fun experience for me as a child.

Those two months were the small break we needed from the torture. It was the only time we had to be reminded we were human beings. These were the moments where you would travel back to when you were stuck in an awful situation at school. I remember in our village always having an abundance of crab every summer. We would hop into our canoes, and there were so many crabs that you could scoop them into your canoe with your oars. The village would gather up on the beach and we would all use a huge cast iron pot to steam cook our catch. Our village would eat those crabs together. I'd be sitting with my grandmother, and she would reaffirm her teachings to me, 'These crab gills, you eat these son. You will be okay. You eat these, and you'll stop wetting the bed.' My great grandmother would be sitting in our circle, confirming what my grandmother was saying to me.

I started training my body on the water when I got older. The entire two months out of the year while I was home, I would be on the lake water. Escaping from it all, out on the water listening to the rippling waves crashing against my canoe. I would spend my time pulling my paddle through the water and I was getting pretty strong. I was getting muscles in my shoulders, my arms, and my chest. I started to build a pretty solid mass of muscle. I figured that I would be able to fend off some of these people. My goal at the time was to be able to fight for anything that I could within the school, with any and everybody, even my own people if it came down to it. My summer training helped me to have the ability to fight, struggle, and get free from them. In the middle of the fight to grow into a stronger young man, fighting my own people became normal. When you grow up with the taunting and teasing from the other kids while receiving these humiliating punishments, you grow a thick skin. There are times that the thick skin fails you and you get insulted enough to fight. No one was safe in their care in this institution.

You learn to take in the sweet moments while you were away. Our parents only had one rule while we were home, be home by dark. We would get lost in the hours of running along the beach shorelines. Just being a carefree child, even if just for a moment. We would fish through the summer. It came naturally in our family as our father was a seasoned fisherman before he became a logger. Our summers were spent surrounding us by our loved ones. My parents made sure that we had time with our Elders, Aunts, and Uncles. The ones that would do their best to pass on important Knowledge. They only had us for 2 months of the year, and maybe two weeks on top of that. We were given the summer, Christmas, and Easter break. With that, my parents made sure to have loving, and safe adults to be around us. We felt secure being home. Having to go back to school was a different form of torture. We'd be forced to go back to school and forced to walk back into their traps.

I was not the first generation of my family that was forced to attend these wicked schools. Both my parents had attended their own industrial schools. These actions within our institution did not seem new to my grandparents, so they provided me with the security I was longing for. All they could do was hug and hold me, give me kisses and more hugs, and try and teach me lessons while I was with them in this great bubble of protection. This was my village, filled with my people, the Ditidaht people. They would show me how they got medicine from the lands, and how it would help the people. That is what they were trying to instil in me. They were trying to provide me with the tools to survive the institution I was being held in.

Leaving our village was always hard. When we would be packing for our trip back, all those ugly feelings would start coming back. Here I was with my family who cared for me, our loving community of Whyac. We had all the support we needed in our village, and we had to leave that all behind again. See you again in ten months, or forty-three weeks. The months were long, and the weeks were longer. When we knew what we were walking into, the travel back to school was never the same as the first one. There were no playful discussions while walking into Port Alberni. We never skipped up the steps up to the school again.

We would drive into town to get to the school. As soon as you could see that building across the Somass River, you could feel the fear creeping in. We would cross the bridge, and I would feel my body start tensing up. My entire body was tightening up and there was no span of time climbing up that hill that would help me relax. When I would peek over at my brothers, I could tell they must have been feeling the same tension I was, the same fear I had. Marching towards the brick building you get a few thoughts running through your head; routines will begin, cleaning is essential, our rights will be diminished, and we will learn our place quickly. Any refuge for normal was felt in compliance. When we listened, we were deemed good little boys.

We would get into the building, and they wouldn't waste anytime it was back into the same old routine. There we were, stripping off our clothes, going upstairs and you get your head shaved. Buzz, buzz. Things got done more swiftly with compliance. We had to accept the fact that we were no longer in charge of our actions. We would be sprayed down with the same chemical substance again; at least this time I knew to close my eyes tighter. On goes our shower with the bar of soap chucked at us. 'Wash up' they bark at us. Nothing new here, just the same old terror. Remember, fear is what alerts us to the presence of danger or the threat of harm and that is what we lived in daily. The towel is thrown in at us, not three, but just one again.

You go pick up your clothes and you still receive the same number. 511, it was everywhere again. Those were my things, and nobody was allowed to touch them because they were mine. Those were the only belongings we had claimed rights too. It was easy to point out the children that were using their neighbours' items. 'You aren't 511. You do not have the rights to those boots. You do not have the rights to those socks. Where's your stuff?' Boom, you were in trouble. You had to take care of your things. Adding tasks to their day was not something that they let us get away with. We kept an eye on our things because we were made an example of if we did not. Our possessions were the labeled linens they provided. That may have been one of the only differences between Hitler's concentration camps vs. the institutionalized whitewashed dismemberment going on here in Canada—they received tattoos for their numbers, and we were able to remove our numbers for two months if we were lucky.

You could always tell who the new kids were in the crowd of kids. Those little bald-headed children would always be grasping at their newfound scalp. They would be hiding their heads shamefully. Walking amongst us all mortified. We were all standing there with bare heads. We were all found in the exact same uniforms, simply different numbers. Everything about this place after your first year was routine. Nothing changed. We did not care at this point; we were all the same. I felt bad for those new kids, that first taste of fright never really leaves you. Our fear just morphs into a different version of fear. With time and experience, you understand the things you need to be fearful of.

School was the same the second year around. We would all go to the same old prayers. We would sing the same old songs. We would all have to say the same prayers in unison. We would have to stare at the same faces that would threaten us. You do this, you get hit. You do that, you get beat. You go out of bounds, you get strapped. We had to listen. We had to do as we were told. Everything had a rule, or a time limit, or a schedule.

By the time I was leaving dorm four, I quit wetting the bed. What a relief. Nobody was hitting me anymore. No more morning strappings; my hands were my own again. Mr. Floyd was in a different dorm room. He was spending his time assaulting someone else now. I was no longer a centre of his daily tortures. I had another aggressor over here. Somebody else ended up hitting me for completely different reasons in this dorm.

Art Thompson & Evelyn Thompson-George

Toddler Art

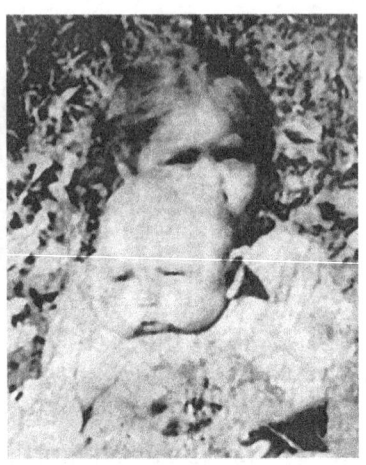

Aunt Nellie with Baby Art

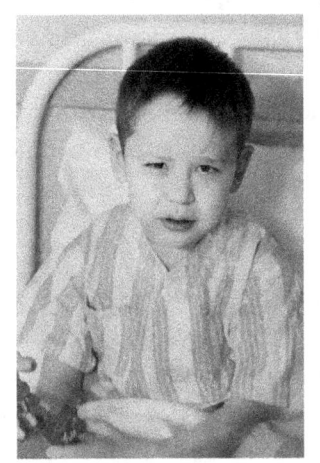

Art in the Nanaimo Indian Hospital

Back: Aunt Nellie, Brother Charlie.
Front: Art, Sister Sharon, Brother George

Pre Teen Art

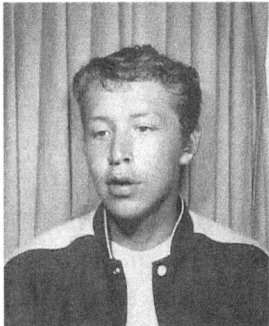

Teen Art

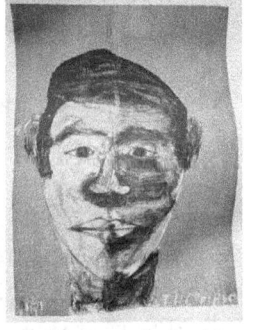

Self portrait during his stay in AIRS

The Defiant 511

Parents – Webster and Ida Thompson

Maternal Grandparents –
Mabel and Elwood Modeste

Paternal Grandparents –
Helen Mary and George Thompson

L-R back: Aunt Flossie, Art, Charlie, George,
Uncle Mike. Middle: Dan and Lou Edgar with
Great Grandmother Mary Chester (Peters)
Kneeling: Uncle Elmer and Aunt Nellie

~ 41 ~

Art Thompson & Evelyn Thompson-George

Airial view of Alberni Indian Residential School,
alongside Tseshaht First Nation and the Somass River

Residential School – 1960
Art found top far right, child beside supervisor

CHAPTER *Five*

Discipline trickled throughout our routines

These stories you are about to read are stories that the general population of AIRS would have experienced. Some memories shed light on some horrific experiences, consequences, and the trauma of those experiences. Abuse comes in many forms. We are born into this world pure, and we are taught how to become evil. Either by watching evil, receiving evil acts, or being forced to be evil. I'm sure there are many other ways to become a monster, but these children did not deserve to live this type of hell. Innocent children, witnessing and receiving pure evil.

Each child experienced some form of abuse within each Residential School Institution. Just being a witness to such cruel acts changes the way you move and the way you perceive the world. Going through even the most basic abuse from these institutions made you hypervigilant. Growing up in a space that leaves you on edge by adults you should trust traumatizes you. These children were forced to grow up quickly because of the way they were being treated.

"Just move on", isn't something new to us as First Nations either. We've always been told to "get over" things. I'd imagine our outward world would feel more comfortable if we were made of rubber and

just bounced back from the way we've been treated. For myself, that won't be the case. I am proud of be here today with the ability to spread my father's story far and wide. The children that would be abused in these institutions would be forced to just move on from traumatic events as if they were not happening. Making it normal to just mask their feelings, or hide how they feel. I hope more of our Survivors start speaking up and letting go of these ugly stories and feelings. This isn't yours to hold onto so tightly.

I was not surrounded by adults that were going to help me

Growing up in this institution we were always told, 'Cleanliness is close to godliness.' This meant that it was apart of our daily routine to make sure this prison was cleaned and cleaned properly. We did not get breaks from cleaning, because every common area was ours to clean. We would have to start with our dormitory, making sure our beds were tightly made. Little forms of discipline trickled throughout our routines. They treated us as their privately trained Privates, and them our Colonel. Our beds looked crisp when we were finally allowed to walk away. You were trained well, because if you did not learn, you were taught through their violence. We were made to understand exactly what they were looking for. Then you would hop into other general cleaning tasks in the dorm, such as window washing, dusting everywhere, washing the floors, and cleaning the toilets.

They were uncompromising with their dusting. Cleaning had to be immaculate. We were tested as children. We would get the white glove treatment from our supervisors. They would walk around with their form fitting white gloves and trace their fingers along the surfaces we were meant to clean. If your job was not done, it showed. If you did not get it done properly, you were going to be in trouble. If you did not do your job, you were going to get hit. If things were not washed, or dusted properly, you were struck. Every surface we had to touch with our dusters were the windows, the ledges, the door frame. We would dust everywhere.

We were kids. We had to do these big jobs with our little bodies. We had chores, well, they called them chores, but it was really forced general labour. I cannot even attempt to call them our jobs because no child was ever paid for their efforts. It was forced labour. Forced because if we did not comply, we were beat. Not complying always led to public torture.

We would have to push these big industrial brooms and scrub the floors with these great big mops. For that six-year-old boy, those mops felt like they were about three hundred pounds soaking wet. Just imagine this little boy swinging that mop about; a cleaning tool that felt three to four times my own weight. When we were unable to complete our mopping tasks, they had more humiliating punishments for us. Everything we could not accomplish to their standards, we would be in trouble, we would be punished, and we would also be humiliated. When the bathroom was not to standard, we would have to wash the bathroom with toothbrushes. Toothbrushes. Six-year-old kids washing the bathrooms with toothbrushes. The bathrooms consisted of five or six stalls of toilets, urinals, and sinks. Every fixture needed to be in pristine condition the first time around. When it was not, that is when the toothbrushes were taken out. All of those fixtures being scrubbed down by toothbrushes, and that toothbrush had to be returned in good shape by the time you were finished. You would do it over and over again until you did your task correctly. Another punishment came in withholding our meals. If we could not do it properly, we were not fed our next meal. With the meals they were serving us, I guess we were not missing much anyways, but the circumstances were the same.

Punishment was always severe, it was not only a conversation of how we can do better next time, but it was also physical, mental, or nutritional harm. The jobs we had were never paid for, but if we did not do it properly, we were paid in those punishments. The payments made to our bodies in forms of hits, slaps, punches, shoves, kicks, pushes, pinches, ear pulls, . They would hit us with anything: sticks, rulers, leather straps, flicks with a wet towel, thrown boots, stones, base-ball bats, pokes with pins, burning my skin with cigarettes, really, anything they could find that they thought would suffice. Anything to get compliance from us.

Those are the kinds of "chores" we had as kids. That is the kind of stuff that I learnt as a little boy. Rules and torture. You did not do your job right? You were hit. You did not eat the meal they provided for you? You were hit. You were caught speaking your language? You were hit. You made an attempt in speaking with the girls? You were hit. They were striking children with all of their power. Five, six-year-old boys, we were getting the crap kicked out of us. Grown adults hitting us with their full force and showing no remorse of those actions. There was no emotion in their eyes when they would hit us. Where they would go in those moments, I cannot tell you. I could not imagine being that adult and tearing apart little kids. Watching the fear in their eyes when you lay blows to their little bodies. Just the thought of it horrifies me.

It is weird growing up this way. You are constantly living in fear of the future. You wake up each day wondering if you can live up to their impossible expectations. You watch to see what is lurking around each corner. Every line up you are required to stand at attention in, you wonder what is coming next. Can I complete the job they have for me? Will I fall short and have to endure today's torture? What are they up to this time? What do I have to prepare myself for next?

This place taught you silence and compliance quickly. I was a bed wetter for many years with Mr. Floyd as my dormitory supervisor, and those morning assaults never slowed down. The fear of being strapped came every morning, and I did not understand how to rectify my behaviour. At such a young age, I was terrified of my own body failing me each night. All I wanted was one day of kindness, and that day never seemed to come.

After one of my first physical attacks laid on by Mr. Floyd, I made an attempt of salvation with our school principal, Mr. Caldwell. Back then I had more confidence in the system I was placed in. I knew as a child that my punishments were not right. I did not deserve this type of violence for my bed wetting. My body was conditioned this way, and that should not be something to be ashamed of, but nurtured. I needed my mother's love, the kind where she could guide you towards the right direction. She would have never made me feel ashamed for my accidents, but she would have cared for me the way she always did.

I went to Mr. Caldwell's office one morning to blow the whistle on Mr. Floyd's deranged strapping on my hands. A beaded strap nonetheless, not just any regular leather strap. It seemed so evil to be so intentional by beating us with something we identified with as kids. Beading reminded us of home, and here he was hitting us with it. Well, I was not going to stand for it, I wanted it to stop. I walked into Mr. Caldwell's office with purpose that day. I told him how Mr. Floyd had been strapping me on my hands, and instead of comforting me from a sadistic supervisor, Mr. Caldwell strapped me himself. I was met with more conflict, and more beatings.

That day I was taught what happened to kids that lie. Mr. Caldwell had brought the boys to attention. All these good little boys, perfectly lined up in their rows. Obediently standing to attention. I stood in front of them all and became the centre of attention for our next lesson. I was strapped in front of all the boys. We were told that it was wrong to lie; wrong to lie about your supervisors. Consequences happened to those who lied, and it was always a public beating.

These beatings taught you how to clam up fast. Reducing your own empathy toward oneself. It taught me we were not allowed to complain. These dormitory supervisors had authority over us children. Our complaining about our consequences was only going to end in more torture. I stayed quiet about my punishments from then on. I went the next few years without my breakfast in the morning for my bed wetting punishment. You see, back then we were punished for our bed wetting because it created more laundry every day. It was a nuisance to them. It was extra costs and time. I created more work because I couldn't control myself. At least, that's how they always wanted to make me feel. I was meant to feel like a problem.

There was hardly any salvation in this institution. No where seemed safe. These attacks I was receiving were daily, so my body was put through the wringer. I would be lucky if I had one full day of no beatings, completely fortunate if there was two days in a row. From my run in with Mr. Caldwell after my first few beatings with Mr. Floyd, I had learned quickly that I was not surrounded by adults that were going to help me.

The brutality of my punishments of bed wetting were dehumanizing. I was hit twice after waking up; first having found my wet bed, and then later on in front of all of the boys. The systematic terror that was set in at a young age was purposeful. When we would get hit in front of the group of boys, they always made a show of it. The boys would be lined up with the smallest ones in the front and progressively got bigger as the lines extended backwards. Someone would have me by the back of my neck parading me back and forth in front of the crowd, '511 wet the bed again today, what are we going to do with him?' Everybody already knew what was going to happen. 511 was about to be brutalized in front of the whole crowd. 511 was about to receive his punishment. In between my hits these supervisors would be making it understood why I was being hit. 'Do you know how much soap it takes to do your laundry?' The hit kisses my skin. 'Do you know how long it takes for someone to wash your sheets?' Another blow to my body.

It was humiliating. They would have us take our pants down and wrap them around our ankles and hit us in front of our peers. All you could do is sit there and take your beating. Fighting against these attacks would always end worse than how they started. Not only would you have to be humiliated in taking a beating in front of the crowd, but you have to endure the degrading conversation of your bed wetting. It was a two-fold punishment each time, beat down twice and publicly ousted each time. You would be forcibly pushed over while they bark at you to bend over.

The way they would have the smallest boys stand in the front seemed so wicked. You would hear the smallest boys in the crowd crying out in expression with each blow. Their stability was being attacked. These adults were teaching the children of this place that if you were not going to comply with their rules and standards you would be punished. It was always reinforced throughout all of these children that were lined up. We were punished often in front of these crowds of kids, it is what helped them with social compliance. When the general rules were not being taken seriously, they showed the entire crowd what happens when you do not listen.

After those beatings, and public humiliations we were meant to just go about our day. It was just a moment, and we were meant to move past it. So, what if you were just strapped, you had to be lined up and ready for your next activity. How is a child supposed to move on from something so emotionally and physically exhausting so quickly? This is where our thick skin came into play, this is where we learnt that our emotions were not a worry of theirs.

When I became more of a senior student in this institution, I would watch as they laid their beatings on those little boys. My mind would wander, and I would catch myself thinking about how I was that little boy not that long ago. Watching these grown men, turn their bodies and swing with their full force towards these kids' bodies. Full force, no hesitation. Every time I did not complete a job, every time I did not finish a chore, I would imagine they would hit me with the same force. Then my mind would think, maybe they hit me harder.

Those hits, every single blow to my little body started enraging the monster inside of me. This is when my anger first started boiling to the surface. Who would not be angry about the actions being laid on me, and countless other children. The anger I had was not a simple temper tantrum a child usually has, this is when my deep-rooted anger towards white people and white authority figures began. It was understanding my place in this institution. We were made to believe that we were lower than dogs. We were taught that we were the savages that they made us out to be. No one before these people ever called us savages, that was a name they gave us. White people were the only people treating me this way, so the anger grew quickly back then.

Rose Carr was a nurse that attended to us as children in the infirmary. She was not one of my assailants, but a quiet woman that would treat my wounds. She was someone who would lend an ear when I would be sent into the infirmary when the strappings were unbearable. My violations were extremely painful. Getting strapped by Mr. Floyd had proven to be the most painful thus far. He had added power behind his hits. Not only was it the possibility of leather breaking your skin, but the added bonus of an unforgiving beaded side of his strap if he felt like mixing it up. There were times that I was not always met with kindness on my infirmary visits. When I would show up to the doorway of the infirmary with sore hands from my strappings there were times that the nurses did not greet me with sorrow. There were times that the nurses would reinforce the notion that we were being strapped because we were bad little boys and would proceed to tell us to soak our hands in icy water.

CHAPTER Six

It was like my body was refusing to keep my soul present

While my dad was preparing for court against his abuser, Arthur Henry Plint, my mom was in the middle of a descriptive writing course for Criminology at Camosun College. My mom helped my dad share his stories in an extremely visual, and detailed way when recounting his memories. These were hard days for my parents, yet it eventually strengthened them and healed them over time. Sharing with each other and mending little broken versions of themselves because they were finally deeply understanding one another. BC Supreme court Justice Douglas Hogarth was quoted after the 1995 trial, "The Indian Residential School system was nothing more than institutionalized pedophilia," he also said, "Generations of children were wrenched from their families and were brought to be ashamed to be Indians."

These acts, these horrific acts were placed and forced on my father through the ages of about 5-13. Through the most impressionable time of his life. These moments being filled with body and hormone changes. Over the years of research put into the development of children, many agree that this time of everyone's life is quite important for your growth and sets you up for your future habits. We come into this world pure and are taught evil. The hardest part about *writing these stories, was stepping away from the computer and continuing a normal life with my family. My children are all varied ages between 4-14, all of the same ages my father was during these stories. I would find myself staring into their eyes, watching the way they moved, and realizing how unbelievably tragic it would be if they led the same life as their grandfather. Writing the stories wasn't as hard for me, it was seeing my father in my children and my heart breaking a little because of that.*

Barbara Rothwell

This institution was a prison of terror. All of this physical and emotional maltreatment on us as children led to extremely low self esteem issues. It would lead to poor mental and emotional health, attachment, and social difficulties. Most of us live with post traumatic stress. Living in panic everyday as a child, having to learn how to suppress emotions, and constantly wondering what was going to happen next were parts of our everyday life. Routines, labour, public torture, 'God save the Queen,' military style direction, the only thing that changed with age was the pedophilia.

When I was about seven or eight years old, I was awakened in the middle of the night. I was half asleep being led out of my dormitory. Why? Who knows, there was no time to question why I was being woken up. We were conditioned to listen on command by then. I have been here long enough, and you learn not to question things. Whoever had me, had me by the wrist going down the hallway. Around this age I had been getting in trouble for hopping the fence to grab some apples to feed myself, but I will get into that later. Well, in my half-blurred transfer I had wondered if I was being led out of bed because of my fleeing. It was hard to tell whether it was late in the evening, or early in the morning when I was jarred awake, but I knew it was while everyone else was still sleeping. I remember because I had to quietly leave the dormitory, while all the other boys were sleeping.

My eyes were still groggy by the time I reached my destination. Even while walking towards this room, I was fighting to keep my eyes open. I was led into a bedroom that evening. It was a supervisor's bedroom. Their rooms were about twelve by eighteen feet. There was a bed, a nightstand, a lamp in the corner of the room, and an armoire that was left open; you could see the clothes hanging from the hangers on the inside. There was light creeping into the bedroom from the bathroom attached to her room.

I was brought to Barbara Rothwell, a female dormitory supervisor. Ms. Rothwell was a heavy-set white woman. She was short with heavy legs, like trunks. A pudgy face, with curly hair. With my memory, that is all I can muster up. As I said, I was pretty tired and was still trying to wake up from what felt like sleep walking. She was sitting there on the only chair in the bedroom, taking up the entire space of the chair. To her left, was her nightstand with a glass and a bottle on top. Her legs seemed partially spread while she was looking at me with a deep stare. The thoughts running through my head were full of wonder. This must be from my going out of bounds in the yard. My behaviour was always getting me in trouble. Earlier in the day, I was punished for hopping the fence for fruit to feed myself. The staff would punish me whenever they saw fit to, and I was punished throughout the entire day for that behaviour. This did not feel any different, this felt like a punishment was about to happen. Another lesson to be learnt.

She sat there looking at me with her fleshy face; jowls hanging. Breaking the silence, she finally asked me why I behaved the way I did. I remember telling her that I was hungry, and that I wanted to get myself apples because of my hunger. She responded with, 'but you continue on with this behaviour. You are always in trouble.' My thoughts were always bolder than my actual answers back then. I thought, well yeah, I am always hungry. I need food. Nobody is giving it to me, so I go outside the fence and get my own food. When I had the pleasure of being home, I was allowed to eat whenever I wanted with no questions asked. I never had to go out of bounds. I never had to hop a fence. I never had to sneak food. All of those things, I got punished for those acts. I was tortured for feeding myself. At home, I was never punished for feeding myself. Hopping the fence for fruit that day is probably why I was standing in front of this women in the late, or early hours of the morning.

She was still sitting there lecturing me on my behaviour. She reaches over to grab her drink, and still spouts more complaints. She goes on about how my behaviour was disruptive, to not only me, but for the other children. They had to stop their routines to publicly shame me for my actions, so it was an annoyance to them. Those other children had to understand that if you leave the fenced area, you get punished. This entire time she is scolding me she keeps reaching over for that glass for the sips she keeps on nursing. The longer I stayed in this room, the more I could smell things around me. I started to notice the smell of what she was drinking. The smell of her drink was offensive to my senses. It was nothing I ever remembered smelling before why that smell stuck with me. When I grew into an adult, I realized she was drinking alcohol. Her body odour, it was so pungent that I could still smell it past her poor attempts to mask it with her perfume.

'Come here,' she said to me. I took a step forward. 'When are you going to start learning to behave?' I stood there in silence. This was far from the first time I have been lectured for stealing the local apples. 'What are we going to do with you?' I don't know. There I was, this little boy intimidated by this big, fat, white women. I have never been alone in a room with an older woman before, so this was all new to me. I did not know what I was supposed to expect. I have never been threatened in this fashion. This experience of having an adult alone in a room with me, while drinking, looking at me the way she was, lecturing me on my behaviour, this was different. I had never had an encounter like this with anyone back in my village, nor my mother's village.

I was stuck and I had no where to go. This woman had me alone in her room giving me this speech about how I need to be a better little boy and how I needed to start listening. Listening meant compliance. So, I would nod my head, yes. I had been standing there long enough to not have anymore words. She reached over for her glass, and she says, 'Here, have this. Take a drink, it'll make you feel better.' I brought the glass to my nose to smell it. Gross, I offered it back immediately. She instantly swung it back in my direction implying I did not have a choice in the matter. I put it up to my mouth and the smell of this drink puts an obvious look of disgust on my face. I drank a little bit of her drink. I will always remember that sensation of it burning as it went down my throat. It did not feel good. It sure did not taste good either.

'Kneel down,' she says to me. Okay, we knelt on both knees when we were in prayer. Okay? Is that what we are doing? Do I have to ask for forgiveness for my actions? I knelt down in front of her. I figured I was about to pray with her. It is really the only thing that makes sense to me. Kneel, pray, ask God to forgive me for misbehaving, for being a bad little boy. As I make myself comfortable on my knees, she starts to readjust her heavy body in her chair. As her legs start spreading wider, she looks at me and says, 'Come here'. What in the world was I in for?

Barbara Rothwell grabbed the back of my head and pushed my child size face into her crotch. No underwear, with bare flesh against my lips. I was a little boy. I was in grade three when this assault occurred. The smell of her crotch was such a horrible smell. I quickly made an attempt at pulling my face away from her vagina, but she grabbed the back of my head even tighter and proceeded to push my face into her even harder. 'Stick out your tongue.' Like the good little boy that she had just lectured me to become, I complied to her demand. I listened to her because she was bigger than me, much bigger. This woman has the body mass to have the ability to really hurt me, so I stick out my tongue. After she was aware of my compliance, she grabbed the back of my head with both her hands. After taking reign of my body, she proceeded to slide my head from left to right. She began to laugh as she was forcing my face back and forth between her thick thighs. She just pushed an eight-year-old little boys face into her crotch and started laughing.

After she was done with me, I got up off my knees and felt nothing but shame. What the hell was going on? No women has ever buried my face in their crotch before. This was something different. This I did not understand. I know a man assaulted me in the hospital, but never a woman. I really did not know what to think in those moments. I was a confused little boy. Quickly snapping me back to reality, I hear her bark at me 'Get the hell out of here. Go on back to bed.' I do not wait for her to give me another instruction, I ran out of there. I ran up a set of stairs, ran towards my dorm, and went directly to the bathrooms. All I could do was spit. Just spit, spit, and spit. I was trying to relieve myself of this taste that was left in my mouth. I'd grab water, gargle, spit again. Nope, this is not working. I reach out and grab my toothbrush and toothpaste, here let's try this. There I was in the dark, brushing my teeth, scrubbing every inch of my little mouth. I needed to rid myself of this taste, the taste of this women. It felt as if no matter what I did, I could still taste her. I could not get rid of the taste.

I felt nothing but deep-rooted shame. How was I supposed to talk about this with anyone? How will anyone understand what just happened to me. I could not imagine talking about it, and telling another person what this big, fat, white women did to me and what she made me do. I stood there in the bathroom that night recounting what happened. The laughter she cried out this evening while she made me lick her vagina, would be the same type of laughter that would pour out if I told anyone about it. Silence, I did not have to tell anyone. This could be my secret. All I had to do was keep quiet.

Gordon Lavoie

Gordon Lavoie was around an average build. He had slicked back, greasy hair. It was black and kind of wavy. He had a moustache and walked around with this debonair attitude to him. He smoked out of a pipe, and that pipe was always carted around with him. He had a little pot belly that hung over his belt and pants. He moved around the halls with arrogance. He had the big man on campus vibes, and he never hung his head low. I can not recall if he was my dormitory supervisor or not. My memory for the positions they were meant to play is not always so clear. I remember him being in our play yard, walking the halls, and him being behind his Dutch doors within his office.

Lavoie would parade around the school halls with his strap always tucked under his arm. Before he would strap a child, he would make a show of it. He would make his strap a prize that he would have to show off and wave about for us all to see. He enjoyed watching our reaction of this tool of mass destruction. I wonder how many children had to endure his whippings, or how many children would coward in fear of his prized possession for that matter. Just a wave of this strap made the kids comply. It was about control, and Lavoie was a controlling man in these halls. He won his control with fear. He controlled me with the strap he carried because no child that experienced it's blows ever wanted to experience it again. To my recollection, he was a supervisor of sorts. He had his own office that was equipped with a Dutch door. The bottom half of his door always remained closed. I remember that there were times where you could see through the cracks of that door. You could peer in if you were close enough.

My mother and father use to bring Kleenex boxes filled with goodies for my brothers and me. I would imagine we were some of the only kids fortunate enough to have gifts sent in from home from our parents. Fortune turned into the devil's own luck very quickly. The gifts so carefully curated from my parents were used against me. These gifts gave these sadists a platform for deviant behaviour. Our treasures from home were never freely given to us the way my parents were led to believe, they were carted away and kept safely tucked away in a supervisor's office or room. My parents would send us apples, oranges, candy bars, popcorn, all these goodies that kids would get enthusiastic to receive. These treats would always be well stocked at home with my parents. We were a family of five and we had three growing boys under our roof with my sister. Snacks were at our disposal, and we were never made to feel guilty for being hungry.

'511, report to my office', you would hear Lavoie's voice pop up over the PA system. Oh boy, this is the time of the day that they hand out our goodies; mine and my brothers' goodies. I would find my way to his office quite excited, at least I would have some type of edible snack today! I would get to his office, and he would shut the door behind me. 'Come over here.' I would walk towards him because he had my goodie, my apple is in his hand. 'What are you going to do for this?' For my apple? It is my apple; I want my apple. Those were my thoughts. I quickly realized that this is some type of game to him. What was he thinking? Why is he asking me what I am going to do? My parents left me those snacks, so they should be mine already. 'What do I get if I give this to you?' I do not know, what do you want? Why do I have to trade for something that is already mine? This does not make sense to me. He wants compliance, but for what? Am I going to comply? Well, I know I want my apple. I want my orange. I definitely want my box of popcorn. He breaks my thought process in saying again, 'what are you going to do for this 511?' Without giving me much time to respond he looks at me and says, 'I'll tell you what you're going to, you're going to do me a favour.' A favour? What kind of favour does this man want from me? I cannot have anything that he would want, or even need. What is a favour to him? Am I going to shine his shoes? Am I going to be taking his dirty linens to the laundry room? No, his favour was going to be far more sadistic than I had imagined when I first arrived with excitement of a treat. 'Come here.' Come here began to become a phrase that would send shivers down my spine. They became words that would be matched with terror soon after. He slowly began unbuckling his belt buckle to loosen his belt. His pants quickly dropped to his ankles with the weight of his belt. There he was, sitting there, bottomless. He was sitting there with his penis out. 'Come here Thompson.' Come here, was no longer a simple act but an act of sheer terror with forced compliance. He wanted me to walk toward his penis or that is all I saw. 'Come on. I want you to play with this.' All this for an apple? I do not think so. You can have the apple. I did not want it anymore. I don't want it enough to have to play with this guy's penis.

My dismissal of his request was met with force. He grabbed my body, held on, and pulled my body in a downward motion towards his crotch in one swoop. He looks down on me with this evil look about him and says, 'Now, open your mouth, and take that in.' Excuse me? You have to be kidding me. No, I really do not want to do this. I have never had to do this for anyone else. I have never had to trade my treats for favours. What is going on here? I was already hungry, but I was not ready for this exchange. Compliance was made, whether it was met forcefully or not. Okay, you will not comply? WHAP. There it is, here we go, I'm getting hit again for not listening. WHAP. You need to comply. Anything this man could reach; you could be met with a hit. He would use sticks, backhands, open hand, anything he wanted. He was not a shy man. His arrogance poured out of him, even behind closed doors. In this instance, the door was closed. In all likelihood, he locked the door behind him.

I learned later on what the word was for the act I was forced to perform on this man. The other kids told me it was called a blowjob. 'Oh, a blowjob, haha.' The other boys told me, 'You gave Lavoie a blowjob', and they would erupt in laughter in conjunction with each other. There was not any pity in these crowds of kids. Looking back now, I would imagine it was because we were all living a similar type of hell in that place. So, all the shame that comes attached to that always followed me around. Lavoie made it really clear who his little pets were. There was a group of kids that he made give him these favours he wanted. I do not know what happened to anyone else, but I knew my story with this man. He would use my mother and fathers' gifts for me to receive my compliance.

His first time asking me for favours were not his last. A part of the humiliation of having to perform forced fellatio, was the immediate rejection of who you were and what you just did. Here I was, supposedly giving him this favour and then he would beat me to the ground because of it. I could not understand it. Why was he treating me like this? Why after getting down on my knees, and pleasuring him, forced or not, is he hitting me afterwards? SMACK. 'Get out of my face. Get out of here!' He was chasing me out and I didn't even get my apple. He did not give me an orange. That box of popcorn was left in his office.

His abuse continued on a daily basis. Anywhere and everywhere on that compound was up for grabs. These meetings were always in secret. I do not really remember if anybody ever watched those things. I am really not sure if anybody ever had access to see what was going on. I do not think any other children would watch through his Dutch doors, but it always felt as if someone had been watching. This man was talked about with the other children. The other kids knew about his blowjob demands. So, leaving his office with the knowledge of his ongoing record with my peers, was completely humiliating. These boys knew his assaults, and here I was walking out of his office every week.

The first time Lavoie anally raped me was violent. Violent because that was not something I wanted to be doing with him. He was forcing himself on my little body. He forcefully penetrated my butt hole and it felt as if my body was going to tear in two. From then on, he continued to force me into both oral and anal copulation with him on countless occasions. Copulation is too kind of a word, rape, he raped me on countless occasions. I would imagine these assaults took place for a year. In this institution, you lost track of how many times these encounters occurred. You do not keep track of those things. It was not something you were proud of. We were not marking these up on the wall to count how many times you have given this guy a blowjob or when he sodomizes you. All I can fathom was it was numerous times over the course of a year. By the time this was happening to me, I had already been losing track of numbers. Coercive control was an effective way to control us as children.

When Lavoie was violating me regularly, I wanted someone to do something about it. I wanted someone to stop him from hurting me. I was often in pain. For example, there were days that I was unable to sit down, from the pain in my rectum area from him ravaging my body parts. I was not able to sit still in class because of the aching pain I was experiencing, which usually led to more beatings. I remember there was a point where I confided in Ms. Carr about one of my anal raping's, because it had been extremely sore that time. I know she was able to offer me ointment for my injuries, but that had been about all she could do. After those few times I would complain about my sexual assaults I decided to change the narrative. I often complained about my injuries related to sexual assaults without telling her how the injuries were caused.

No one has a working check list of how to move past these types of offences as a child. Healing from such traumatic events takes time, and we never had time in these institutions. We were supposed to be made of rubber, you know, bounce back. Compassion is not something we were offered in this school. We sure did not receive compassion from the school workers. Compassion was stripped from us and if we mustered the courage to share our story with another child, we were usually laughed at.

Ed Kempling was our school's minister. From previous experience in religious people, I was made to understand I could trust this man. My only other experience with a church before this was with a genuinely nice man that lived in our village, his name was William Wickerbee. He was a very consoling and understanding human being. I remember confiding in him with the issues I had at school, and the understanding he had. He would wrap his arms around me. He would feel remorse for me. I admired that man. To my understanding, he was the United Church Minister. My mother would take me to his church in Clo-oose. She would take me to that church against my will, but back then it was more about the triggers I felt then the church itself. I knew the man that worked inside was a kind and compassionate man. He did good work for our people. When his name comes up, William Wickerbee, I have nothing but good things to say about that man.

Having had William Wickerbee as such a caring influence of a church man, I thought my encounter with Ed Kempling would lead to a similar relationship. I thought I could trust the man with my secrets I was made to bury in this institution. I had complained to

Kempling about being, what we called 'bum-holed' at the school because he was a minister. I thought I could confide in him, and he would keep my secret, or show me a little compassion. He seemed to be a reasonable person and would listen and show grievance for me. To my knowledge, he did not do anything about the complaints I made to him. Just open-ended, almost meaningless conversations that never changed anything, other than being able to get it off my chest.

When I told Kempling about being butt-holed, he asked if it was one of the other students who was doing that to me. At the time, I trusted him enough to be honest with him and I told him the truth. When I had complained about Lavoie, it had been because of the frequency of his violent rapes. My rectum was sore, and it was becoming unbearable on my little body. Kempling's soft responses were, 'Well, we will see what we can do about that.' He made me feel reassured by his comments. I felt safe in those moments of baring my heartaches on his man. He was someone I felt I should be able to trust. The situation did not seem to improve after discussing my rapes with him.

We had another minister in our school with the name of Hoops. He was another man that I would confide in about my violent rapes by these grown men. I remember telling Hoops about Lavoie's aggressive behaviour and Hoop's reaction was fairly similar to Kemplings'. He would say things like, 'We'll have to get to the bottom of this' while acting very reverend-like. He would make comments like, 'In Gods eye that is wrong,' but the situation would never change. They would always lend a careful ear, but I would always be met with empty promises of change.

Rudy Brugger

Rudy Brugger was a tall man, as least to us kids. He towered over us. He had this short brush-cut hair. His sides cut short, shaven army style. He wore khaki outfits and black leather boots up to his knees. Those boots were constantly meticulously polished. He had a bulky frame. He was a heavy-set man, but still muscular. He had larger arms and a big healthy chest. He was quite a bit bigger with his stature compared to us kids. Brugger always had a distinct accent, but one I could not put my finger on as a young child. Growing up and listening to people as an adult, I realized that he had a German accent. He would strut around with his two-foot cane tucked under his arm. He would walk around as if he were a drill sergeant. He would conduct his daily business this way as well. His orders were always barked out in military fashion. It was as if he was working a guard forces job, waiting to be called out on duty.

'One, two, one, two, one, two, three,' we would be marching into the dining room to his military marching call outs. We were organized and walking in a rhythmic way forward. 'One, two, one, two, one, two, three.' Here we are, in line for that awful cod liver oil, squirt. 'One, two, one, two, one, two, three.' Marching towards class, being shuttled to our next destination. Marching, marching, marching, everywhere we go we are marching. He enforced many military style practices on us as children, and marching was only one of them.

Brugger was unforgiving when it came too our bed making practices. When he told us he wanted the sheets pulled tight, it meant those corners better be tucked away properly. He always wanted it to be made so tight that if he flipped a quarter on it, the quarter would bounce three feet in the air, and he would finish with a quick swipe with his hand to catch it. He would walk down our rows of beds doing his quarter check on a daily basis. Checking the beds with the bounce of a quarter. FLIP. If his coin did not bounce those three feet, you would be found with a stripped bed to try all over again. You were only granted that one chance to correct your mistake. If you could not have that bedding tight for the second walk through you were going to be punished. If you had to try for a third time, even more punishment. Those punishments were not only held in the dormitory, but in that line up of boys they liked so much. Always the smallest boys up front, to the biggest in the back. Lined up and spread across like a band choir, so everyone could see said punishments. This time, I was a little bit bigger. I was not in the front rows now. That is when you really noticed the echoes of the youngest boys' gasps when the strap landed on the skin.

My punishments with Brugger were focused on my running away or what they classified as running away. He would take me in front of the rest of the kids and say, '511's a runaway. He's never going to learn.' I would be hopping the fence to get fresh apples off the local trees. I would come back, and he would catch me. He would beat me after I crossed back into the boundaries and would always drag me in front of the group of boys. They were always making a point of instilling that fear into the children for compliance; social compliance in a group setting. They always wanted to show the boys what would happen if you tried leaving this place without permission to do so. Over the years of my attendance, I would begin running away from this place. I would start leaving past the apple trees to escape. They always seemed to find me, and it was always the same outcome. I would be getting back to the fence and Brugger would hit me with an open hand, a back hand, or anything he could grab. The order would be the same once we reached the basement, pants down with a strap to my bare bum.

Brugger was a systematic asshole. He was disciplined and liked things in order. He was uncompromising and meticulous. Another thing I remember about this man was his afternoon trips away with students. I always remember as a little boy watching a select few of my peers getting to have afternoon rides into town. They would have the chance to leave this place with Brugger and they would come back with this happy experience. They got to leave the school grounds for the afternoon. I remember it happening at least several times before. It made me bitter knowing it would never happen for me because I was a troublemaker. I would run away or cross the fence. I would always be out of bounds or talking to the girls. I was always caught doing something, so I was always in some kind of trouble. I knew I would never get those kinds of favours from Brugger because I was a bad boy.

The Defiant 511

One day I got a call over the PA system. '511, report to the office.' I made my way to the office and to my surprise Brugger was there waiting for me. '511, how would you like to go to town with me today?' Of course!!! Excitement, that is all I felt. What does a kid do, you know? You get to get out of this place, get out of school for a while, get to make a trip downtown, maybe socialize a little bit. It was unknown and exciting. You get to get away from the school and that made it a thrill. I was practically skipping with joy headed to the car. I jumped into the car feeling like I won the lottery. I just wanted time away from the school, even if it was just for a short time. I wanted to experience what those other kids were able to experience when they would come back to school happy from their days off campus grounds. I was excited to have fun. I wanted to feel that.

Of course, as a little boy you get excited about the whole trip. I got to leave in a car; strapping myself in and buckling up to start the engine. Lap belt was secure and down the road we go. Brugger decides to start up some small talk. Sure, this is different. 'First time to town 511?' Yeah, other than my parents getting me. We are driving the streets of Port Alberni and it all looks really nice. Peering out my window and taking it all in. Driving past all the buildings and admiring all the different store fronts. Everything looked different that day, it was a different view when you were able to enjoy a day off of that hell hole. The scenes were different here. In town there were people walking the streets. I saw laughter and families were out. I saw men, and women walking. Everyone seemed busy. A day out on the town, watching all the cars zooming by. It was nothing I was able to experience before. Driving through town on a busy day, it was different.

He parked the car in front of a building I didn't recognize. I am thinking, well all he said was we were going to town, what are we doing here? 'Get out of the car' he says to me. I was becoming very obedient when orders were given to me, so my responses were pretty immediate. I jumped out of the car. I have Brugger's full attention now that it is just him and I, so I know I have to pay attention. After I get out of the car, he starts leading me up this flight of wooden stairs to this building. We get to the top and walk through a door to this room. There is a window that overlooks the Alberni Canal. I could see the mills with smoke pouring out of the chimneys. Out on the water had passing boats, and big log booms. Down below the window you could see houses. Wow, this was amazing. You could see so much from up here. I had never been to this part of the town before.

I really felt privileged. I felt privileged to be there as a little boy looking out this window at a different view. I was actually feeling pretty happy. Here I was, on a day pass looking out at this beautiful view. It was all so exciting, to be chosen when I never thought it would be possible. I sat there in wonder — is this how the other kids felt when they were gone for the day? Is this what they got to do? Did they get to peer out at this view too? Was it another view? Of course, they did, they must have. This, this feeling I had was happiness. I was happy to be overlooking all of this stuff, all of this commotion going on in this waterway view. In the meantime, this man is walking around, strutting around his apartment. Something is different this time, he is drinking something. Chug-a-lug, chug-a-lug, up goes this brown bottle. He keeps taking long drinks each sip. I did not know what he was drinking, but I now understand he was drinking beer. Nobody had ever drank beer around me, but Brugger was having one. One led to two, and two led to more. He looked over at me asking, 'How do you like this 511?' This is great, I like this!! I kept admiring my view out the window.

Hell was taught to me at that early age. To my understanding of the term Hell, we heard preaching's of hell being a place you go if you were bad. It was a place you ended up. Hell is where your soul goes for eternal punishment in the afterlife. Well, in those fleeting moments of feeling complete and udder joy, happiness, and privilege, they were met with feeling as if all hell broke loose. It felt like I was going to go to hell. With a slap of reality, I began to believe that this was my hell on earth. '511, drop your pants and take off your clothes' he barked at me. Was I confused? You bet. Was I scared? Yes, I was very scared. I was terrified because I was isolated and alone with this man. I had wondered what was going on in his mind. What is he going to do to this naked boy? He wants me naked and alone. I am getting hit with instant terror. I am afraid. I am scared. All of these things are racing through my brain and red flags start popping up everywhere. I am becoming overwhelmed with my surroundings. It keeps popping up in my brain that I am very alone. I am alone in this room with this man behind a different locked door off campus and in his personal space.

My clothes are coming off. My pants are down. I am complying. 'No, no, all of it.' I peel off my shirt. Next are my socks and shoes. Off come my underwear and my undershirt. Everything is gone and I am left standing there completely naked. There I was standing in front of this man, alone. What is this all about? I know what this is about, or at least I think I do. I remember what has happened in the past, is this going to be like that? He is still drinking. He is just standing there smiling at me. I am scared to look out the window now. All those moments of joy have diminished. I am afraid of turning my back towards him. He is kept in my view, so when he turns, I turn. Otherwise, I am a statue, I am not moving. This is becoming extremely daunting. He moves, I move in accordance. I slowly start to try and cover my naked body with my hands. Why is he just making me stand here naked? What is going to happen? He cracks open another beer. He is keeping me afraid, and I am scared. Still following his every move, he is not giving me any hint of understanding. He just keeps drinking his beer. He finishes another and replaces it just as quick. This time, he slams that one down. Finished in one gulp it seemed. Now he is ready to talk.

Here we go, another lecture about my behaviour. 'Why do you keep running away? Why do you continually go out of bounds?' I am hungry and I know there is fruit trees out of bounds 'Why do you continually talk to the girls?' I need companionship. I have a sister on the other side now. I would say hi to her and I would be in trouble and get hit for it. For just checking in with my sister, my younger sister. He starts asking me, 'why do you want to visit those people? You are not allowed to visit them. We have got rules, you know them. You've been here long enough.' So, I answer him, I do not know. His response was, 'when are you going to know?'

'511, get down on your knees.' In an instant he is screaming, 'GET ON YOUR GODDAMN KNEES!!' I dropped to my knees. I am terrified. I know my eyes are big, because I am watching this big burly man in front of me and he's standing over me with his little whip. He is still fitted with his black polished boots, his khaki outfit, crew cut, and his face is snarling in my direction. I have complied because in these horrified moments I just want to be a good little boy because good little boys do not get hit. I am terror struck in position. This would be one of the first times I remember praying. Here I am, reaching out to God. I am saying a prayer in my head, God, please help me. This is not going to be good. I am scared. Please, help me.

'GET ON ALL FOURS!' He pulls out a gun and puts it to my head. I feel the metal against my head. He cocked his gun. CLICK, CLICK. Instant panic shoots through my entire body. I slowly start moving my body down into position. I am on my hands and my knees, complying. I am going to listen. I stay down, in position, the way this man wants. I am not moving for anything. If there is an earthquake here, I am still not moving. This guy has a gun on me. I remember what guns can do, the power they have. Guns had the power to kill, and I still did not know what this man wanted with me. I know they hurt, I know they maim, I know they kill. I am going to comply because I do not want to die today.

He left me alone like that for a few minutes on all fours. He walked around the room still drinking. He would sit down just to admire his view, this nice vista outside of the window. He would randomly giggle, or chuckle while looking at me on all fours. Laughing at my compliance. He has me so scared that I can no longer move. I am stuck still in fear. Exactly where he probably wanted me to be, full of fear. I was so afraid of moving that I stopped watching where he would move. All I could hear was the springs of his chairs squeaking when he would sit down and the release of the same springs when he would stand up. I could hear him get up and walk around.

My eyes were fixated straight ahead. Even when he left the room, I was stuck still in position.

When he came back to the room his footsteps were accompanied by another sound. There was a repeating click and clacking sound echoing on the floors. It was not another person, I understood at least that much. I was still too afraid to move my body. He had a dog with him. 'I'm going to teach you a lesson on how to be a good boy.' In my experience of lessons with this man, I knew I had the right to be terrified. A lesson? What kind of a lesson? What was this dog going to go? Why was it here with us?

He brings this dog beside me, and now it is standing on my left side. The dog stares into my eyes. This dog is a big German Shepherd dog, light brown and black, panting heavily beside me. He is looking into my face, and I'd imagine he sensed my fear. We have met, he is looking into my eyes. Brugger gets down beside this dog and starts stroking the dog's penis. He is getting him sexually excited. The dog's physical response is happening, and his penis begins to stiffen in response to his touch. He starts talking to the dog, 'do you want some of that?' He begins laughing. Laughing. I am panicking in these moments. I am thinking, how the hell do I get out of here? Can I run? Can I make it out of this place? No, I cannot. I am trapped. He has a gun, and a gun can kill me. I am trapped. I have no place to run. I have no place to hide. Can I fight him? No, I do not think I can. Brugger towers over me, he has a gun, and now he has this German Shepard with him. What is he going to do? Is he going to sic this dog on me? All of these things are racing through my mind.

I started silently crying. I was being held captive in an isolated room, naked, with a man who is teaching me a lesson with a much bigger dog. When he successfully had the dog's penis erect, he helps the dog into position on my back. The dogs' paws extend out on my back, and it pulls me backwards when it extends its nails into my skin. With the dog's erect penis, it begins to penetrate my anal cavity. This dog is raping me. A dog. When I tried to get away Brugger took his gun and held it to my head again. In a calm and direct fashion, he says to me, 'Keep still. Keep still you little bastard.' I am going to keep still—damn rights I am going to keep still. Keeping still hurt, it hurt a lot. I could feel the claws of the dog on the sides of my body, digging in with what I would imagine the pleasure it was feeling. His pleasure was matched with excruciating pain. Pain on my sides from the pressure of his claws, pain in my knees from baring the weight, pain in my rectum from being penetrated repeatedly by this animal.

How the hell am I going to live through this? What the hell was happening to me? He has a gun, and I am not allowed to move. My compliance was rewarded with rape. I wanted to die. I came to this place to be raped by an animal, a dog. This, now this was painful. This was the moment where so much changed for me. I remember being that little kid thinking, you can have my body, but you sure as hell are not going to touch my soul. I am lost in those moments of pain, unaware of how long it lasts. My only memory that was left was the pain I was feeling. The claws ripping into my skin. The memory of feeling that dog's penis enter my body. It felt like my insides were going to rip apart with each stroke. It was an eternity. 'Get up and get the hell dressed.' And that was that. He waited for me to get myself together before we left his apartment. We left and he acted as if nothing happened.

Nothing looked the same on the drive back. It was almost like all of the colours turned into a black and white movie. I was glancing past all the faces. It was like my body was refusing to keep my soul present. I was floating above myself lost in moments I wanted to forget. In a state of blank thoughts while racing against a stranger on the street. Sitting beside a man who just finished raping me at gun point. Not a normal rape but a form of beotiality. How was I going to pull myself up to have the energy to survive. We walked through the doors of the building, and he was met with nonchalant questions from his supervisor buddies like, 'how are you doing?' Meanwhile I am the little kid that is suffering. I was just anally raped by this dog, and he does not seem to give a damn about what happened. I was angry. Angered to the thought of how he could separate his actions, like it was just another day. I did not go to bed as instructed. I went to the shower with no care as to the consequences of not listening. I do not give a damn; I was going to have a bath. I was going to try and clean my body after this stinking animal was on me. I wanted to scrub hard enough to get rid of this, this feeling I had. The longer and harder you scrub, the easier it is to realize that this physical stuff can go away but it is the memories that burn in. You cannot walk away from a memory like that. That memory walked with me the rest of my life, along with the scars that the animal left behind.

From that moment on, when I had to interact around a dog it made me physically panic. I would try and avoid that feeling because I know it affects me. My body starts reacting to this big dog around me, and I start getting the chills. My body starts sweating and I feel it under my arms and on my face. Unnerving panic, uncontrollable and so debilitating. Forty years later, and my body is still responding this way. The actions of that day led me down a road where I would abuse animals. For myself, it was because of that panic I would feel around them. I would hurt animals to protect myself. After years of that panicked response, I would try and correct my behaviour, but the fear would never leave. The scars still lay where that animal dug in his claws. After that day I never trusted Brugger again. We were never going to have that buddy, buddy type of encounter again. He was not salvation of a day away; he was terror behind his disciplined German demeanor.

Arthur Henry Plint

Plint was short in stature. He had salt and pepper speckled greyed hair that was usually greased back. He did not always dress particularly well, not like the other dormitory supervisors. His pants would be greasy from wearing them for too long and his shoes were not really kept clean. His body odor was rather pungent. Being close to him, you could tell he did not care if his body odor was offensive or not. He had such an unnatural walk to him. He did not walk upright, but more in an ape like walk. He was an adult, someone that always seemed bigger than me. He was someone else I could not fight off.

Plint was also an alcoholic. There were many times that he would walk around reeking of booze and stale cigarettes or cigars. He was a really repugnant, ugly little man.

Brugger and Plint were one in the same type of person. The only real difference between the two was their appearances and how they held themselves. Brugger was a strict enforcer who stood to attention, and who's boots remained polished at all times. Where as Plint put no effort in his outward appearance and was always hunched over in some manner. I was frequency being violently raped by both of these men. I remember when I would have two, or very rarely three days in a row of not having an encounter with these men, and well, that was a good week. These men were monsters. They would be beating me with all of their adult strength, and it was as if they were getting off on the physical assault aspect of it all. They must have felt a lot of power behind their hits. When they were finally done with their physical assaults, it would always turn around and become a violent rape if we were left alone. Their rapes with me were always anal or forced blowjobs. It was sadistic, their pleasure peaked when they were hurting me. Holding back those screams in those moments was incredibly difficult, but you caught on after so many encounters because you would see the switch from punishment to pleasure for them. They seemed to enjoy the screams, and the torture aspect of it all.

I hated the Alberni Indian Residential School, so when I grew older, I would run from this place every chance I got. They labelled me a runner at a young age, but back then I was just hopping the fence for some fruit, now I was trying to leave and never return. When I would transfer to an older dormitory, you could tell the supervisors must have had some type of conversation about my behaviour. I used to imagine their conversations behind closed doors, 'Thompson has an attitude', or '511 has an attitude', or '511 runs frequently so you have to keep an eye out for him.' When dormitory staff would do their change over, you would be forced to have a conversation with the new staff. Just by their demeanor alone, you knew they knew your history.

When I was about ten, our class was being taught about the evolution of mankind. We were being taught that man originated from ape-like ancestors and that made the group I had been sitting with giggle. How funny we thought. How does that even work? To go from a monkey to a person. The differences at the time seemed so drastic of a change. Well, unfortunately for us boys, Plint heard our laughter. We watched him storm towards us in anger, while he wondered why we had the audacity to be laughing during a lesson in class. After he barked at us for our response, I remember looking up at him and telling him it was because our teacher had just told us that we came from monkeys because of evolution. That was all it took to have this man fly off the handle and become infuriated. This is the type of situation that landed me a strike to the side of the head, with my ear taking the bulk of the pain. The force behind his hit would make my ear ring, which caused my delay in hearing when he screamed at me to report to the principal's office. Since I did not jump to attention and move quickly, Plint yanked on my ear dragging me the entire way. He was painfully pulling at my ear out the building, across the field, into the next building, up the stairs and all the way down the corridor to the principal's office. My thoughts during this experience could add up to one question, what the hell is going to happen now? How humiliating, being dragged like some disobedient animal. When I was reprimanded by the principle, he beat my bare bum for calling Plint a monkey. As far as I was concerned, that is not what happened, but if the shoe fits wear it, the man hunched over enough to see the similarity. The principle would further his yelling at me by telling me that "I should always listen to Mr. Plint, especially when given orders". My response was probably too subtle for him, but I was being honest. I told him that I could not hear Plint, because you know, my ear was ringing in pain from him smacking me too hard. Well, being to the point honestly just landed me in more trouble. The principle met my honesty with another strike against the head with a yank of my ear saying, 'What are these for?' Just added humiliation and pain.

Lavoie may have been my first assailant to lure me to his office with the promise of my goodies from home, but he certainly was not the last. Plint would take a page from Lavoie's playbook and use the same tactics on me. Plint was my dormitory supervisor, so his office was on our dorm floor. His office had a desk inside, with a file cabinet, and a closet to hang his coats. His office had the same type of Dutch door that was fitted at Lavoie's office. The top door swung open so you could look in, but the bottom door was usually shut so you could not actually go in. His bedroom was off of his office, so his two rooms were interchangeable. I would get that call over the P.A., '511, report to Plint's office. You have a letter.' I remember the excitement of having a letter from home waiting for me. We thrived on contact from home because our contact was limited. While we were in school, we would get the occasional phone call or letter. We were always longing for that connection of comfort and hope while we were essentially trapped in this child like prison. They would lure me to their offices (that were also their bedrooms) with the understanding I would feel that connection through my letter or goodie. My parents still sent those boxes of treats to us. Just more ammo for them to isolate us for more unwanted torture. Growing up in this institution, I remember wishing my parents would not bring me those treats. I used to think it would subside my assaults by these maniacs. My parents just wanted us to have these treats because they knew what we were living through, they also went through these institutions. They knew in their silent way what type of life we were forced to live. I would imagine they thought it was comforting. Those supervisors made sure we paid for those treats. Plint was one of the men that milked these treats for all of their worth. I was getting daily messages to head to his office for treats or letters. Those visits were never quick. They never ended with a hand over of anything for free. Those visits would always end in some type of abuse. Those abuses were either sexual (anal rape or having to give him a blowjob) or physical (beat me senseless). There were also numerous times where I would have to leave that man's office with absolutely nothing to show for it.

Our bodies always seemed to be under a microscope one way or another. At a young age, and all the way through my stay at this institution, I would receive countless rectal inspections. Why, you ask? To be honest, I am not quite sure. Not all reasons had to be given to us back then. Back then we just listened and did as we were told, otherwise we had consequences to match our disobedient behaviour. Our rectal inspections were given to us by our male dormitory supervisors. I can recall back to one inspection that I received from Plint; I stood there quietly as per his request. He would then insert his finger into my rectum, and he would not stop at that discomfort alone. He would then further his hold on me and grab my pyjamas while forcefully shoving his finger farther into my rectum cavity. This forced me to raise my body on top of my tippy toes in pain, making a failed attempt to get away from him. The pain this man was inflicting on me was too much to bear and I began to scream out in agony. Only then would he release his grip from me and let me go. No apologies, no remorse, his only response was 'You should learn how to keep still.' That meek little boy responded back with a quiet, Yes Sir. The quality of these inspections never improved over time. When I was about ten, I remember another inspection I was forced to have with this man. This time the pain was so excruciating. I was in so much pain from the forceful way he stuck his finger into my rectum. It felt as if he were trying to rip my guts out. That pain lasted for a few days back then.

I have always made an attempt to have a good attitude when it came to life. I enjoy making people laugh. As a young boy, making people laugh usually came at the cost of having a little sarcasm. So many boys grow up with this cheeky, sarcastic attitude about them and I was not different in that sense. One day for one of our lunches, we boys were served with an under cooked, and rather disgusting macaroni and cheese. I was sitting with my pals that day, laughing about our current mess of a meal. That was not so different, we always had gross meals put in front of us that we were made to eat. It was always something, whether it be a poorly cooked or heated meal, not enough to eat, or a diet of food we were not accustomed to. The only difference in this incident was that Plint heard our laughter. Our laughter came from a remark I had just made saying how we were having the most delightful dish in front of us. Without warning Plint shoved my face into my undercooked food. Only after having my face covered in this disgusting meal, which was now oozing off my face, did this man even bother to ask why we had been laughing. Of course, by then the lunch hall had already caught notice of my altercation, which now was matched with public humiliation. Discipline time. Off to the principal's office I go again. Time to be strapped on my bare bottom, yet again. Plint added to this torture after my apparent discipline. He towered over me and demanded I eat three additional plates of food aside from my own plate. Four plates of food is what I was made to consume. Four plates of one of the most repulsive meals they offered at this place. There was no chance to explain my laugher because he never gave me the chance. My punishment left me feeling so sick that I wanted to vomit up this dreadful stuff. As I was meant to choke it all down, I remember thinking to myself, Man, I wish I were big enough so I could cram it down his throat. It was a growing need, or want I guess, to make him suffer the same way he would make me suffer.

I remember during my counselling, incidents of my learned mannerisms from this institution, such as keeping one hand on the table at all times, no talking at the table and no laughing, to name a few. I had to remember that these were learned habits that I was inflicting on my children and grandchildren. I can close my eyes and still see their sad faces followed by an eerie silence. The air would remain tense as we all practiced the silent treatment. No one would talk because of the fear to further any tension. This was an easy trigger for me, it would suck me back to that feeling of being a little boy and understanding their fear and confusion. Those moments are some of the constant reminders of Plint and people like him.

Using our language within the walls of this institution was always a huge no, no. It had been a long time since I had been in trouble for using my own language in school. With each passing year the ability to use my own language diminished little by little. There was a sheer terror instilled at a young age to make any attempt to use my fragmented comprehension of my own language. Being caught speaking any language but English was an immediate punishment from whichever staff was around in that moment. In Ditidaht, we have this word, Mum-multh-nee, it's meaning—white man. There was a time that I found out that in Ohiat language, Bub-thald, was the same meaning. I was so fascinated when I first found out, how cool, a word with the same meaning but with different pronunciations. How funny, I wonder how many different ways you can say white man. I found myself laughing aloud. I was lost in a funny coincidence of words. Always found in ear shot, Plint would hear my laughter. He must have had some type of fun radar because he always seemed to catch me. Well, he quickly glided over to my side to ask me, 'What is so funny?' He knew I wasn't allowed to repeat my language. It always seemed as if the supervisors enjoyed catching you in a lie. They were always testing you in these immature ways. I decided to remain silent while cowering my hands raised to protect myself. There was a point where under his supervision you would learn that you never had the right answer, regardless of the question. Everything seemed to outrage this man. He would find himself in a rage with my silence and it was met with the exact response I initially feared. Plint would proceed to drag me by my ear, quite painfully, to the principal's office. Of course, I was interrogated upon my arrival, what did you say they ask. 'I don't remember.' That was my response, I do not remember. You are at the point of your survival that you must try everything to limit the amount of pain you know is unavoidable. My avoidance was met with threats. The principle would raise his hand that had his strap wrapped around it. Just the sight of that thing would raise your hairs on your arms. He makes the fear worse by saying in an evil tone, 'Perhaps this will jog your memory.' In hopes to avoid a harsh whipping I shouted out, 'BUB-THALD!' Well, what does that mean? How did I even put myself in this situation. In this situation where I have to tell a white man, that I am saying white man in our language. I tell him what the word meant. After I explained myself, I knew to prepare myself for the inevitable. He would begin striking me up and down my left arm with his strap. While he was acting out his deranged behaviour, he would be screaming at me, 'You should never make fun of us!' When Plint came to retrieve me, he would greet me with an open hand to the head. Not stopping there he furthered my shame and refused me my next meal.

Long after the Alberni Indian Residential School was closed, I remember seeing this former principle on the street one day in Port Alberni. When I realized it was him on the street, a devilish grin danced on my face, I was going to engage in a conversation with him. 'Hi Bub-thlad', I was no longer his student, and I wasn't afraid of this man. His response was illuminating, 'what does that mean anyways?'. At that moment, I realized that my linguistic lesson of the past obviously didn't work. When I realized he hadn't paid attention when I taught him the first time it led me to my next question, 'why did you beat me so much at the Alberni Indian Residential School?'. I was curious if he would be honest with his answer. His response was, 'It was all part of the disciplinary plan'. The disciplinary plan. He answered honestly. What a spineless man. We were kids. I turned around and walked away in disgust, hoping to never see him again unless it was in a courtroom. Unfortunately, I never got that chance.

As a young boy whenever I ran away from this institution my first stop was always the Tseshaht Reserve. I would have to walk through the reserve if I ever wanted to walk across the bridge to get to town. There were times where I would be caught on this reserve as I was trying to escape. Let me tell you about one of those times. One of the members from the reserve held me captive in their home while they called the school to issue a report to say they had a young boy that ran from the school. I was retrieved by Plint that night. I can still remember the stench on this man's breath while we walked towards his vehicle. He had already been drinking alcohol by this time. Plint literally threw me into his vehicle. He was visually annoyed that he had to stop his plans to come and grab me. I could then hear him mumbling under his breath. I hear him complaining about my bothering his evening. Even though the school was only down the road, that would not stop him from pulling the vehicle over to lecture me. Just another lecture about how I need to listen better, how I should not be running away, and of course, how I need to be a better boy. This is when it went from a normal pick up to just another nightmare. Plint would go on to tell me that there were ways we could come to a satisfactory resolve, if I was willing to comply to his wishes, his next manic plans. This man's satisfactory resolves were only satisfactory for him, and I would always have to cope with his demands. I was curious at first and I had wondered what could warrant me a more lenient punishment. How funny to think, a more lenient punishment, there was no leniency in any punishment I've received in this place, with these people. That bad breath stench he had came from the green bottle he had been guzzling. By the time he had finally finished every drop he would dispose of the bottle by chucking it out the window. Tossing the bottle out the window alarmed me with the shattering of the glass against whatever broke it. It was then I decided to take it upon myself to offer a form of gratification he had already been used to from me, some irrational form of sexual gratification. In those times between him and I, that meant I would provide this pathetic excuse of a man a blowjob, or I would fight less while he anally raped me. This made me sick. How has my life led to this point of having to offer this psychopath sexual favours in hopes to not get beaten to a pulp. How can offering my body up to this man make the pain less? Other then an orgasm, what was this man getting from me? I guess my willingness to comply so quickly enraged him because Plint would just snap after my offer. Maybe he was thinking the same thoughts as me. In his drunken state my vocal compliance made him crack and now I was about to receive my punishment. With a closed fist Plint would start punching me all over my body, he would focus on my face, upper body, and my legs. He would switch from a punch to an open-handed slap every once in a while. Drunk, angry, and maybe confused about my willingness to comply, he made me pay for that willingness. My body was in so much pain from the blows he laid on me. My little body tried fighting back. I was trying to defend myself in what little way I could at the time. My childhood strength was no match to his aggressive adult stature. He overpowered me and continued to strike, slap, punch, and thrash every square inch of my body that was made available to him. Just another beating that would last for an eternity. When he finally decided to come up for air from his aggressive mental break, he would start his vehicle engine and return back to the school. We would walk into the building, and I remember suffering in agony with each step I took. My face was bright red from the recent assault, and my body was covered with countless bruises. I was sent to bed, just another evening at the Alberni Indian Residential School. That next morning was no different and that same routine of fear had to be brought forward. I was to be made an example of what happens when you run away. Just because I received a body numbing assault the night before, it did not prevent Plint from continuing his lesson for the other students. Here we go again, another public flogging on my bare rear end. This assault was met with Plint screaming, 'and let this be a lesson to anyone who tries to run away!' I remember being that little boy cowering in the front of the line up. I remember the feelings I felt when I would watch these supervisors publicly beat on our peers. I can still hear the gasps of these poor souls up front and the muffled moans they would let come out. There was always that constant fear swirling around this place. We were always forced to watch these grown ups beating up little kids.

There was never really much of a pattern of when Plint would lay his assaults. The time of day did not seem to be the issue for him. The only thing that seemed consistent was the isolated aspect of his behaviour. The majority of my rapes I endured with Plint were in his room. Supervisory staff had offices with rooms attached to them. This is what would give him the ability to choose when he would assault me. If there was someone around the surrounding area of his office, he would just usher and shoo them away and that would be that. It did not matter; he always found a way. I was made to experience an assortment of different sexual assaults with this man. To name the types of acts, there was aggressive anal rape. I would have to give him blowjobs. He liked receiving hand jobs, and he enjoyed giving them out himself. There were frequent times he would fondle, grope, and feel my body. He enjoyed kissing me on the mouth. It was always about feeling that sensation, the entire event would be filled with touch and lips, all of these unwanted advances. Advances that were made at such an early age. We were being forced to be sexual before we even understood the healthy version of being sexual. We were made to be sexual beings in an unhealthy manner. I would grow up with the wrong sense of understanding of what a healthy sexual relationship should look like.

These were all foreign feelings we were forced to experience at a young age. We were enduring adult sensations when we were only children. It sure messes up your understanding of these things. Not only was it scary, but more often than not it was extremely violent. We would be receiving this torturous action and version of sexuality, and then it would be abruptly met with a completely different set of fears. They would finish their torture with threats of our families. Now they would add the aspect of our parents well being if we were to speak of their tortures. So many children would clam up in fear of loosing the only warm connection they would have. They were threating the life of our parents if we spoke up. We were not allowed to talk to anyone about their abusive ways.

By the time I hit around the age of 12 or 13, Plint would make me one of his most repulsive offers he would hand out. He asked me if I wanted to be one of his boys. Well, I did not really understand what that consisted of. It was confusing to me. Well, what do you mean? We were in an all-boy dormitory, he was already my supervisor, so I was stuck with him regardless. Why would I choose to be this man's anything? He would ask me again; do you want to be one of my boys? He then made it more clear that he meant he wanted me to exchange favours for candy bars, or the letters my parents would send me. He was known for that behaviour amongst us boys. He would ask certain boys to carry out certain wishes for him. He finally gained my attention when he mentioned he would leave me alone in the process IF I helped him with what he wanted. Leaving me alone meant he would not be raping me anymore. The trade off was that I would be the boy who would have to take the other children to him so he could rape them. I would be leading a younger boy to the same type of rape I endured with him. He wanted me to take a younger child to be raped, to sacrifice them for myself. What in the hell was he thinking? I had no angle to come from to make this make sense. It was not right. I did not want that. I did not want to be the boy to lead a terrified child to this monster. I flat out refused his sick offer. He was pissed. In a strike of rage, he would proceed to turn his big ring inward and smack me open handed to the head. After the strike rang through my head, I felt the force of my legs giving out and he had me on my knees. Forced oral copulation on him was the less of evils he would make me endure. He was a brutal man, and I would comply to avoid more physical abuse. The fact of the matter was he was still much bigger than me, a grown man. I did not have the strength to overpower him, so compliance led my survival.

CHAPTER Seven

"Do you have jurisdiction on an Indian Reserve?"

One of the most empowering moments after any abusive relationship is when you take your power back. As children one of the only ways you could experience any form of power was when you stepped over those invisible boarders. Running away was a form of empowerment.

The intention of running away was never coming back. Yet, for so many of these children they would always be carted back one way or another. My dad was brought back by the RCMP, family members, and AIRS staff themselves.

We were in Snuneymuxw

My residence was at the school, but when I hit the middle school age I started taking classes at A.W. Neill School in Port Alberni. (A.W. Neill School was named after Alan Webster Neill. Neill was a former mayor of Port Alberni from 1921-1945. More interestingly, he was also a former federal Indian Agent for the West Coast of Vancouver Island. This also meant that his job was involved in the operation of the Alberni Indian Residential school. In 2020, the School district 70 Pacific Rim voted to change the name of A.W. Neill elementary *school to Tsuma-as elementary school. This choice was celebrated through the neighbouring nations within Port Alberni)* This meant that I was leaving the school grounds weekly at this older age, which opened up more possibilities of running farther away from this place. I had these friends from Nanaimo, Les Thomas, and Gary Manson. They were my classmates at A.W. Neill, and we planned an escape. We planted ideas in each other's brains that we were going to do it. So, it was all premeditated. We knew what we were going to do. We knew what the plan was. A.W. Neill was close to a set of railroad tracks. Those tracks would eventually lead out of town. It had to go somewhere out of the valley. I remember that is how I got here from Duncan, so I knew the tracks could stretch a far way.

Les, Gary, and I skipped class one day. We got off our bus and went straight for the railroad tracks. It was eight thirty in the morning and we showed up with purpose. We walked and walked. We circled down the Alberni Valley and kind of headed North. Then the track would start bending and we would be headed in a southeast direction. The tracks were leading us out of the Valley. We were getting pretty tired by now, and it was starting to get dark. We were up around the Cherry Creek vicinity. I started telling the other boys, 'We need to get off these tracks, it doesn't seem like we are getting anywhere.' We had been walking all day and we had only made it as far as Cherry Creek. So, we started checking out our surroundings. In the distance we could see these cars driving by. The cars were racing by actually. We realized they were going up a hill that would decide whether you would be leaving the valley or heading in. It was the local highway. We made a calculated decision. We were going to cut across all of the fields in front of us, then through the bushes, and make a beeline towards the highway. It was getting darker by the time we were making our way across those fields. We would end up hopping fences, bushwhacking through the bushes, and crawling under barbwire fences, whatever it took we were getting there.

We finally reached the highway. Here we were, these three kids from the Alberni Residential School, out on the highway. We stuck out on the side of the road like a sore thumb. If the wrong person would come across us our punishment back at school would be severe. We were lucky that night. I always remember feeling that way, so lucky. The first car we had seen came to a stop. You go through all of these emotions when you see the parked lights brighten. Am I going to be in trouble? Is this someone from the school coming to haul us back? Then come the hopes. I really hope it is not someone from the school. The car door flung open, and it was my relatives! Welcome faces of Sandra White and Lorraine Good. I do not know who the driver was, but they were the best-looking faces I had ever seen. We practically jumped into their car. We knew before even hopping into the car that they were headed to Nanaimo because that is where they were from. It was a nice trip to Nanaimo. We shared many laughs together in that car. Many were spent laughing about our trials and tribulations about walking along the railroad tracks. I remember we were all hollering in laughter over seeing all the excrement on the railroad ties. The trains had all these holes in the boxcars, and this is where the passengers on the train would defecate, and it would drop onto the tracks. We would see those piles and think, oh man we still got a ways to go. We were in the company of people we trusted, and it was so welcoming. Everyone was happy. We were giggling. We were on our way to Nanaimo. It worked! We made it out of Port Alberni. There was not anyone that was stopping us. We were gone.

I remember getting to Nanaimo and feeling pretty good. Nanaimo was my maternal grandmother's homeland. We were in Snuneymuxw. These people were my grandmother's people, all of these people in Nanaimo. I would take time to visit my family members when I got there. I went to visit my uncle, Colby Good. 'Arthur, what are you doing here?' I ran away, and you know what? I was proud of that. 'Why, you should get back to school. You know, you're going to be in a lot of trouble.' Yeah, I didn't care. I responded very matter of fact, 'I'm not going back!'

I stayed with Les Thomas and his dad for about two weeks from what I recall. Every time a police officer came to the door, I will always remember the old man looking at the cop. The cop says, 'I've come for your son, Gary Manson, and Arthur Thompson. Are they here?' This guy was straight to the point, 'Well, two of the boys are here.' He would be so nonchalant about it. The cop would respond, 'well, they have to come with me.' His response was my favourite part. 'No, they don't.' He said no. He just said no to the cop! I was shocked. The old man followed that up with, 'do you have jurisdiction on an Indian reserve?' The RCMP officer looked down to shake his head. He was caught in a hard place and this old man was going to force him to walk away empty handed. 'I didn't think you had any. Now get off my village! Get out of my village! Get off my steps and get off my land! Get off the reserve, you have no rights here!!'

What a turn of events. You could not imagine the kind of feelings that I had in that moment. My experiences with the RCMP were to get in the back of their squad car and get shuttled back up to the school, always, it never mattered when I would confide in them about my abuses. Then here was this old native man who was telling the cop that he had no business there. I felt proud to even know this man. Things were looking pretty good. Every time they would come out, they would get turned away. We got brave enough to wander out on the reserve. We never left the reserve boundary because we never had a reason to. We had all kinds of food. We had family there who fed us any time we walked in their doors. There were clothes there for us. Casual clothes, not our numbered uniforms from the school. That was a nice change. Every place we would go, we were fed. I would go visit my uncle Colby again and they'd feed me. 'Aren't you scared of somebody catching you here?' No, Les's dad will take care of it. My confidence was building from watching this old man take care of our problem with the RCMP. No problem, he made them leave.

One day who did I see walk into the village? My grandfather, Elwood Modeste, my mother's father. What a welcome sight. I ran up to him and gave him a hug. Geez Grandpa, what are you doing here? He looked at me and said, "Well son, I had to come talk to you." Curious, okay what do we have to talk about? He says, "Well, are you going back to the school?" I thought it was obvious by now that was the last thing I wanted. I told him, no, I am not going back. He tried to continue on talking, but I stopped him right in his tracks. I would say again, no grandpa, I am not going back! He responds with, "Well son. One of the things that you have to remember is that school has control over you. That school has control over wherever you go, and you are accountable to that school. If you stay out of that school, what's going to happen to your parents?" Geez, I did not think of that part. I was enjoying my freedom. I was enjoying the good meals. I was enjoying not being beaten and raped. He continued on explaining, "they're going to charge your parents a hundred dollars a day, that's a lot of money." That is a lot of money. I added up over a thousand dollars quickly in my head. I took his word for it. I had no need to not believe my grandfather.

'Come on son, you can come back to Duncan with me. We'll talk about it on the way.' I trusted him. He is my grandfather, and he always looked after me really well. All of the people in his village would care for me and he was at the top of my list. He says again, 'come on son, let's go! We'll go back to Duncan.' Sure, I guess. So, I got into the car. My grandfather turned over the engine and we were on our way. We were driving down the road and we only got a little way up the street, and I could see something at the edge of the reserve. Someone was waiting at the edge of the village. Sitting there at the edge was a policeman and Plint. What was this? I looked over at my grandpa and said, you knew this was going to happen, didn't you? His response broke my heart. 'Well son, I'm really sorry but they made me do it. They phoned me and asked me to come and get you.' I felt instant and deep betrayal. Now I start to lose trust in my own people. They were using my people, my family members against me. Old man Thomas did not bend at their will, he was stronger than that. They did not retrieve Les Thomas or Gary Manson that day. I was the only one that had to go back, alone, with Plint.

As Plint was driving on the highway back to Port Alberni I realize I really need to go to the bathroom. We were rounding up to Cathedral Grove at the time and I knew they had a pull-out area there. So, I figured I would give it a shot and I asked to stop. I need to go to the bathroom; can we stop so I can relieve myself? Plint responded in his gruff voice, 'hurry up, I can't wait here all day.' He kept mumbling on, but I stopped listening after I heard I had the go ahead to leave his vehicle. I thought, what a great opportunity. I am not afraid of the woods. When I was at home my parents, they taught me how to be in the woods. They taught me how to be on the water. They taught me to be by myself in the outdoors. They taught me to not be afraid in the woods. I was not afraid of Cathedral Grove.

I made a run for it. What do I have left to lose? I may as well make a break for it. Well, unfortunately Plint knew something was up. He came chasing after me. I just so happened to trip and fall. What awful timing. He caught me after I fell, and he had me by my neck. He was not even giving me a chance to walk this time. He was dragging me by the scruff of my neck all the way back to the parking lot. Interesting, this is going to be a nice trip back to Port Alberni. To add insult to injury, I still had not gone to the bathroom. I told him, you know, I still did not go to the bathroom. 'I don't give a damn!', was his response. I immediately chose defiance. I had just come back from two weeks off of this man's torture, and I was in a cheeky mood. I was witnessing this cool old Indian man shooing away the local RCMP. He has already done everything he could do to me, so why not push the envelope. He doesn't give a damn? Well, I will show him. I thought to myself, okay, what do I do in defiance? I wet myself. You will not let me go to the bathroom? I will piss right here in your car. I am going to pee myself and get it all over your car seat. I am on a mission to piss this guy off. I mean, I thought it was rather humorous. We were already starting the climb back up the hump to descend down back into Alberni Valley. It suddenly dawns on me, he has been drinking. Actually, he is currently drinking. Great. Just my luck. I do not know what he's drinking, but it doesn't smell great. He seemed to be getting in a better mood. I guess the alcohol was kicking in.

We did not go directly back to the school that night. We start heading up Mission Road and then stop at the three-way fork in the road. The left-hand side would take us back to the school, but the centre and right go towards Tseshaht village. He pulled his car into the driveway on the first house on the road on Tseshaht's reserve. It is this old, tattered, unpainted home. I knew this house. I know the people that live in here. I know the Dick family lives here because I had family throughout this village. The Tseshaht village is where my grandfather's mother was from. She was a Shewish. Shewish's lived down the road from this house. So, we knew the neighbourhood as kids. We knew who our family was. We were raised this way as children. We were taught who our (extended) family was. It was Thomas Dick who lived at this intersection.

Plint made me sit outside for a while. 'Stay in the goddamn car. Try and run away. I'll catch you. I'll beat you.' To be honest, I was tired. It had been a long day. I woke up that morning enjoying a free day in Snuneymuxw. I did not know how long it would last, but at least I woke up happy that morning. I would have never thought that I would be stuck here in Plint's vehicle by the end of that same day. I guess all good things must come to an end. So yes, I am going to stay. Sure, I am tired. Plus, my pants are wet. If I go anywhere with a soggy crotch people will just laugh at me. So, what the hell I guess I am going to stay.

I have no idea what is going on inside of this house. It sure seems to be taking long enough. I wonder how long Plint is going to make me wait. I would imagine he is making me wait in my soiled pants to suffer just a little longer before he takes me back to school. Plint came outside and opens my car door. He grabbed me by the arm and forcibly pushed me inside the house. He was prodding me, pushing me, and shoving me the entire trip in. His clumsy behaviour had me tripping all over my feet while I found my way inside this house. He shoved me in a corner and made me stand in it.

The room we were in was not painted. It just seemed very unkept. It smelled and the dishes were overflowing in the sink. The table was full of wine, beer, and whiskey bottles. Just an assortment of booze bottles filling up the kitchen table. Then there were these two guys sitting amongst this mess. They were laughing, joking, and having drinks. They were having this good ol' time and I was meant to just stay in the corner. I was standing still beside these set of stairs that led upstairs where the bedrooms were. I do not know what time it is, but it is dark out. I am getting tired, and these guys kept on drinking. I was starting to fall asleep in place while they kept drinking.

Dick jarred my sleepy state by calling me over to the table. He called me over with his own language. I'll always remember that because he did it in front of Plint. No repercussions happened. Dick knew where I was from. He knew who I was because he knew my father's name. He knew my grandfather. My grandfather's name was well-known in the Tseshaht village because of their connection with Chief Shewish. I got up, curious as to what he wanted. Here's this big burly native man. He was unshaven with salt and pepper scraggly hair. He was really unkept, with these ugly clothes on. He was calling me over in this native language. I get up and go over to him. I am walking over with no fear. He is a native man who knows my family. Plint is still sitting at the table continuing his drinking. Dick looks at me and says in this gruff voice, 'I understand you're a runaway.' The corners of my cheeks began to turn up. My cheeky attitude starts making its way through and I'm suddenly proud of my accomplishments the last two weeks, and even those of today. I guess this is my opening to have a fun conversation with this native man. So, I smiled in response to his question and said, yeah and to my shock he hit me. He hit me. He gives me a backhand across the face with his left hand. He knew his stature, and he put his weight behind his blow. He stood a whole head above me and his arms were more then twice my size. I was a kid and he was a grown man. He is this big burly man. A strong man. I later find out that he was a longshoreman.

I felt that blow. It felt as if my whole face was going to break away from him hitting me. I reeled back and I did not fall. Somehow, I managed to keep my balance. He snarled at me, 'what the hell are you smiling about?' What the hell just happened? Did, did that just happen? Did this man just hit me? This is crazy! Here is a native person beating me up, someone who knows my family, and he's asking me what's so funny about running away from that school. I am confused. Is this a joke? I did not answer him. He raises his finger and begins to curl it towards him, 'come here.' So, I go over to him. While walking towards him I quickly size him up, and you understand the power he has against me and my much smaller body. I am pretty sure I understand everything I need to know about this man by his actions. Here I am thinking, he's a native man, realistically him and I should be getting along. It does not seem to be working out in this instance.

He grabs me behind the back of my neck and he smashes my face into the table. I remembered hearing those bottles just jiggle that were on the table. Some of them fell off. 'See, we're going to teach you a goddamn lesson about running away.' And I'm quick to question this so-called lesson. I am thinking, what kind of lesson have I not learned. If I could take those other punishments, I can take this one from this Indian guy. This guy does not know what these other animals have put me through. All of this happening at the kitchen table and Plint is still sitting at the table watching. My face is still against the table. The skin on my face begins to feel as if it is stretching across the table from this man pressing down so damn hard. It felt like my eyeballs were going to pop right out of my head. My ear was burning from being pushed down so hard. I was gaining a pretty hard mind at this point. Hard because I was getting stronger. I was teaching my mind to block things out. It did not matter to me. What could they do to me that has not already been done before?

I do not know which one of them did it, but one of them stripped my pants down. I knew there was something terrible that was going to happen here. Two big men, both pretty intoxicated from whatever they were drinking while sitting at the table. They lost control. I had seen Plint drunk before, so I knew what to expect with him. I did not know this other guy, this Thomas Dick. My face was still against the table but now my pants were down, and they were laughing. A shared amusement I would imagine. Next thing you know somebody was pouring some liquid down the crack of my bum. That liquid went on for a little while and I could feel it running all the way down my legs. I thought, boy, this is not going to be good. So, I started flailing. I gave it everything I got with my arms with my face against the table. What came next, was one of them hit me in the back. POW. They drove their fist right into my back and knocked the wind out of me. I was gasping for breath. It was hard enough having my face pinned against the table, but to have my breath knocked out of me as well was a lot to take. That's when I decided I wasn't going to move. Somebody just hit me so damn hard that it felt like my ribs were going to break. Maybe they did break. I do not know; I was just lying there confused at this point. What in the hell is going on? That is what was racing through my mind. And then I start to feel, feel something starting to happen. Somebody took my rear end cheeks and is starting to spread them. They were being held open and then pure agony of quick and deep penetration. Somebody was anally raping me right then and there.

After a while I felt another hand grab a hold of my neck, while the other one released their grip on me, they were handing me off for somebody else's turn. I do not know which order they went in, and I do not even know who was holding me down in the first place. All I did know was they were sure a lot stronger than I was. They had their way with me. I remember crying and the tears that rolled down my face. I remember, you know, wondering why the hell or what the hell was going on here. I remember thinking about that as this was happening and trying to conjure up a prayer. How am I going to get out of this? What kind of God do I pray to? What kind of god did they teach me to pray to when I was in that school? Apparently one that makes this stuff happen, that is who. He does not help me. Nothing helps. I am crying and nobody pities me there. I am hurting, I'm screaming like there was no tomorrow. There is nobody there to help me. My prayers go unanswered again. Whoever was holding me pulled me off the table and they slung my body against the wall. 'Get your fucking clothes on' he snarled at me. Gladly, I will gladly do that. I will gladly put on my clothes. It then dawned on me. These men just had their way with me and then threw me aside like I was a piece of garbage. They got their satisfaction from me and then threw me aside.

To make matters worse, we still need to go back to school. My night is not over. When we walk through the school doors it is already getting pretty late. Plint is smoking a cigarette feeling pretty arrogant as we walk through. I am limping through the halls. My side hurts, my face hurts, my back hurts, my legs hurt, just everything about me is just one big mass of ache while I was walking. We get to the principal's office and here comes the lecture from him. Why do you run away? Why do you do this? Andrews was quick to pull out his strap. I did not give a damn from there on. I had endured a lot worse by then. I stuck out my hand and then I pulled it away when he brought down his strap. I could see a rage brewing in his eyes. I am feeling pretty defiant. He starts hitting me with that strap. He misses my hand, so he gets up and I could see his blood veins just bulging. His face turns red, matching his carpets. He is mad, and I understand his madness. I understand his rage. He starts swinging that leather strap anywhere he can land a hit on my body. Just hitting with all of his strength. I just curled up in a ball and I ended up on the floor. He is still hitting me and now Plint joins in. Plint is kicking my ass. I knew it was Plint because Andrews couldn't land his hits and kick me at the same time as hard as he was.

When they finally feel as if they were done teaching me this lesson, they allowed me to go to bed. I do not get to bath to wash away the filth off me that these guys left behind. They force me to go to bed. I have to wait for morning to get rid of that. To try and get rid of that filth. I went to sleep angry that night. How dare them send me to bed this way. I had not only wet myself in defiance, but I was raped twice and got the shit kicked out of me by two grown men. That next morning all of the kids got up to shower. When I was able to get under the water, I began trying to wash off those men. Trying to erase that stuff from my memory. All of that animalistic behaviour from the night before. It is kind of hard to let those things make a quick exit from your memory when it only happened the night before. Then I would begin questioning myself. Did this actually happen? It seemed like such a short space of time in between so many events.

Hmmm, nah, it didn't happen. Back then, you would have to get used to forgetting about things like that relatively quick. Then the supervisors would bring you back down to reality and bring it all back up again. It was time to manage this score in front of all of the other students. Here we go again, everybody lines up. There I was, front and centre again with my pants down. They would be talking about 511. 'What happens with 511? Why are you running away?' My only answer I give them is, I do not know. What I want to say is, I don't like this place, but I do not know, is the best they will hear. I would get hit for another infraction. 'Oh, you're starting to swear now. Aren't you the arrogant boy?' I suppose I am, after those two weeks away I am getting rather arrogant myself. I am not nearly as strong as these guys yet though. I know maybe in a few more months, or another couple of years I'll be strong enough to take them on, but not at the moment. They still have the control.

They beat me in front of all of the kids. I remember being in front of all of the little ones that were down in front. I was standing there with my pants down, bare ass with my penis hanging out. You could see the scared look on all of their faces. I remembered what I was like to be that scared little boy in the front, but now I was the defiant one. It did not matter to me if I was getting hit on the butt. I am all up for that, I've been there for a few years already and I knew what that was all about. It was about the routine, and it was still the same. You still had to yank your pants down and stand in front of all those kids for your public beating. You still had this guy up front blabbing on about 511. This supervisor up front droning on about whatever infraction that happened that brought me in front of them. I know what this is about, it was about teaching all those other boys a lesson too. 'Bend over 511.' I will bend over. Smack across the rear. You could hear all the kids in the front row gasp. AGAIN. Every time they struck me, they got a reaction from all these kids. By then, they were not going to get a reaction out of me, not anymore.

'You're not even worth it'

Growing up caged in a child like prison did not stop the regular flow of life for me. I was getting in trouble for so much already and talking to the girls across those invisible lines and boundaries was always one of them. There had been a point in my adolescence where I would become more interested in girls, like most boys my age. The natural flow of life was happening with my escaladed life style at this place, and dating was a form of change I wanted to welcome. Finding compassion in a young girls' arms was something I would long for. Compassion in any sense of the word would be nice. The only compassion I was granted at the time was during those months when I was allowed to see my parents, my village, and my people. There was a young girl across the fencing that I had grown fond of. Her home was located on the Tseshaht Reserve not far from this institution.

One night, in October 1963, I would make a break for it to go enjoy a date with my would-be girlfriend at the time. We met during one of my apple raids outside of our guarded fence of that institution. I was caught, by her father, Thomas Dick. I knew this man, and he knew me. He already broke my confidence a time before. Running into him was no such luck that night. I could only imagine how the night was going to end now. He was intoxicated, and drunk people made me nervous. With my experience of drunk people, it usually meant that they were more open to being far more physically violent. His eyes were blood shot, and he would proceed to stare at me with a drunk squint to his eyes. His lips would remain partially open with a hint of drool pouring from his lips. He seemed dirty, and his face did not represent a clean shave for some time. I scanned the room he confined in, and you could see all these empty bottles of beer and wine scattered on the kitchen table. The kitchen was still unkept, and bottles seemed to be freshly cracked open and consumed. Thomas Dick would push me forcefully into his wall and he would threaten me by saying, 'Stay in that fucking corner until Plint gets here, you little shit.' Just the mention of Plint's name, rolling off the tongue of this delusional human being would send shivers down my spine.

While I stood in the corner living my own personal terror, I would hear the footsteps of the girl I risked it all for. She was coming down the stairs and I was not the only one to hear so. Her father whipped his head around to bark at her, 'get the hell to bed!' She matched his screams with her own, sticking up for herself she would say, 'I'm going to the bathroom!' In her own way, she was really checking in with me. I would imagine this was not the first time her father had been intimidating while he was drinking. She quickly turned to me to offer advice. She whispered quietly to make sure I listened because 'he'd get pissed off' if I didn't. She made sure she did not waste any time in the bathroom, and she would run up the stairs to her room afterward. After she scurried upstairs Plint would show up.

Plint matched Dick's intoxication with his own, showing up to his home reeking of his own booze. When Plint walked through the door, he would say, "You again? You never learn, do you?" He would reach out and smack me upside the head again, with the usual force. You would think that was that and we would be on our way back to the school, but this was different. Thomas Dick was Plint's friend, which meant we would be sticking around for a while. Plint joined him at his filthy kitchen table and began to enjoy each other's company, drunk and laughing amongst each other. Even though both these men seemed intoxicated enough, this is where they would enjoy what they called their night cap. Neither of them required more consumption of alcohol, but here I was watching them guzzle more alcohol down. I remember standing there obediently in the corner while they poured back a 26'er of whiskey and several beers. More alcohol in their system meant that they were becoming more brave with their anger. Plint was angry I was running away, and Dick must have been angry that it was his home I was running to that night. A conversation of my running would obviously come into play and both these animals would agree that 'I should be taught a god damn good lesson.'

Another lesson. What have I gotten myself into. How was I going to be tortured this time? Both of these men would bark in my direction to come and join them at the table. My previous experience in this home had me nervous beyond measure. I had already been cornered into this situation, so the only thing left that I was able to do was to comply. I quietly moved towards them in fear. When I complied, I thought I would be met with less violence because I was listening. My stomach was in complete knots because I was trapped in a room with two intoxicated men. Who knows what courage they had just mustered at the end of a bottle. Thomas Dick would then proceed to grab me by the neck and slam my face into his unkept kitchen table, again. The force of my face landing on his table would cause the bottles to rattle about again, a sound that remained a familiar noise. In those next quick moments, I could not tell you who ripped my pants down to my ankles because of the angle that my head was being held in. The right side of my face was being shoved into this filthy table. I could move it to catch a glimpse of the horror I was about to endure. I was not this scared little boy anymore because of my previous experience in this home. I had a feeling I knew what was about to happen next, so I started to fight against this. I started kicking my legs around. I balled up my fist and started swinging hoping to land a hit on either of them. That hope of getting away was declined dramatically after I was met with two blows to my back. Whoever it was almost hit my spine. Those blows successfully knocked the wind out of me and it left me gasping for air. By then my pants were already off; they had won this battle.

I was at the end of my rope when I felt something stinging my rear end. One of these men had poured some liquid over my rectal area while the other was holding control of my legs. I have but a second of time and before I knew it, I am in excruciating pain. A piercing pain that shoots through my body as one of them begin to penetrate my asshole. Forcefully, and quickly ripping through my body. The pain runs through my body not skipping a beat. You could fight, but it has happened so many times before that you learn not even that is worth it. You learn to grit through the pain and let them have their way with you. When you fight, you are physically beaten down until your fight is diminished. They have their way with you because that is simply their goal. I lay across this repulsive table absolutely mortified. Through all of this heightened pain, it was met to another high of the feeling of the next man jump right on in after the last man finished his climax. Feeling his sexual gratification for mere moments to be met with another ruthless erection entering my backside. More cause for my body to want to rip to shreds.

One of the only ways I found I could survive this torment was to mentally escape. Cringe your eyelids closed and hold them tight. Escape. Leaving my own body to escape these adult men ravaging my child size body. Letting their drunken state be a cop out for their animalistic behaviour. I thought to myself, they can have their way with me, but they will never touch my spirit. I was brought back to reality at the end of the next climax. He threw me to the floor like I was nothing. In the moments between he would be catching his breath grasping for air. That is all you would hear after they were done, the heavy intake of air being pulled through his throat. He would then look over at me and say to 'get the fuck dressed.' My trip back to school was spent in tears and trembling in pain. You choose to become numb. You look past everything in those moments. Lost in the thought of, will this bullshit ever end?

Plint ripped my arm towards his after our car ride. He led me all the way up through the building and he brought me straight to Principal Andrew's office. Here comes round two with these assholes. This is where my defiance starts peeking through again. I stuck out my hand for Andrews and as he was about to swing back to land his blow, I pulled me hand away from him while sharing my most devilish grin. I was already in trouble anyways; I may as well have fun with my punishment. They need to know that they cannot get to me. All hell broke loose, and Andrews fell into a pit of rage. You could see his rage grow with the red blossom that ran through his face. The blood veins would quickly become visible on the sides of his neck and his shirt collar seemed to pop up to attention. I really pissed this guy off. His anger was bulging, and he was about to burst. His anger erupted and he would begin to take his strap and flail it in any direction. Its only course was to end on my body. He would be belligerently spouting orders of extending my arm for my strapping. He would start swinging, and I match his actions with moving my arm. Here we go, now let us add in that Thompson grin. I was choosing not to take it anymore. I was done. After the night I had, it was time to mess with them. Man, he went nuts. Not only was he taking his anger out of me, but Plint would join in on the assaults. There we were two grown men making very valid attempts to hurt my body. I was getting hit, and kicked, and strapped all over my body. When I would try and cover my body, they would just match it with hits elsewhere. I didn't care; I was in a defiant mood. I gained the courage to spit at them, like they had done to me so many times before. Go ahead, let's see how they like it. Well, they did not like that at all. It sent them into an even higher state of fury. I hated the fact that I was back there. They must have felt big that night. They laid their dominance out of this young 13ish year old boy. A child becoming a young man.

I was humiliated having to return to this hell hole again. After they felt I had an adequate beating, they sent me on my way. I went to find salvation in a bath. When I removed my clothes, I stood frozen to look at my body in the mirror. All I could see were these red marks all over my body. I could not see my back, but I certainly felt it. Lumps were found all over my head. I remember lying in my cot that night thinking, one of these days I am going to get even with these bastards. I remember an extension of my punishment was that I would have to remain confined to my dorm through the next few days.

As kids we use to watch across the river towards River Road from our dormitory room, or really any window with a view. Anytime we would see a taxi go by it either meant that there was a visitor coming to the school, or there was someone going into the neighbouring village. A lot of us children would wait in anticipation to see if it was one of our people we knew that would come out and visit us at school. Well today seemed to be my lucky day. Maybe all that pain I endured was so my luck would turn around in the morning.

My dad hopped out of the cab that morning. Here I was, confined to my dorm room and I see my dad get out of the taxi that I had been recently daydreaming about as it was driving down River Road. I was not allowed outside, but we had these windows that would only open enough to stick your face against it and yell out if you wanted to be heard. You could not stick your head directly out of it, but an opened window seemed to do the job well enough. I saw him get out of the cab, so I rushed to pop open a window. He was walking up the stairs and I yelled at him. He whipped around searching for where he heard these yells, so I yelled again and stuck my arm out the crack to wave. He finally noticed where I was and said, 'come on down.' I told him I was not allowed because I was being confined to my dorm. Annoyed and I'm sure confused, my dad would start talking under his breath while he continued walking up the building's front steps. He went inside of the building, and it wasn't long after that where I saw him. He had come inside looking for Plint. Plint was still my dormitory supervisor at the time, so he was the one who ushered my father my way.

Plint was wearing his other mask at this time, being the courteous school worker for my father. My father was here to visit all of us, myself, my brothers, and my sister. Plint wasn't going to argue with my father, so he opened my dorm room, and we were made to go find my siblings after he picked me up from my dorm room. As we were walking down the hallway my dad put his hands on my shoulder unaware my body was covered in bruises from my rape and punishment from the night before.

This institution was so calculated, they gave me all long sleeve shirts, and pants to cover up my bruises. I guess they figured if I had them covered it would prevent me from talking about it. Well, my father caught on rather quickly when I winced away in pain. My knees buckled from his touch. My body was responding before my mind had time to catch up. Of course, this led to my father asking me, 'what's the matter?' I responded with, "Well you probably already knew I ran away anyway. Well, they caught me, and I got beaten." My father decided he wanted to see so he says in a concerned voice, 'well, let me have a look.' There we were standing in the hallway of the school, and I pulled my shirt out of my pants and undid the shirts buttons. I can not imagine what my father must have felt looking at my body in that moment. He saw with his own eyes the amount of torment those men left on me to heal from. He got a good look at all the bruises on the front and the back of my torso. In that moment of sad reflection, he proceeded to ask, 'who in the hell did this?' I came this far; I may as well be completely honest now. I told him the truth, Andrews and Plint did this after I was caught running away and brought back to the school. This was my punishment for running away.

I still remember the way Plint hid behind his locked door. He would cower behind his door, unwilling to talk to my father about the punishment I received from him. It was nice to see he could be afraid of someone else. My father chose to yell through the cracks of Plint's locked door, 'If you touch any of my children again, I will personally take it out on your hide'. I was stuck in a daydream of what it could look like if my father was able to get his hands on him that day. I imagined what it would be like if he was able to carry out his threat, the same way Plint always carried out with me. My father was a stalky well built man with incredible strength, burly and muscular like many hard working loggers of that time. He would have been able to exact his revenge on Plint for what he did to me if he had the chance.

Boy, was my father mad. He stormed off down the stairs. He was on a mission. Someone was going to pay for the brutality laid on his child. He made his way to the main hallway in which the administration offices were found. The principal's office was bigger than our supervisors and with him being the principal it warranted him a secretary. This young lady was sitting there behind her desk displayed in front of Andrews' closed door. My father found himself pounding on her desk in anger, demanding the presence of Andrews. Wow, my dad was going to do something about this. Right on! This is going to be different. Someone was sticking up for me within the walls of this institution. Andrews opens his door and floats over with this debonair principal mask on. 'Oh, Mr. Thompson. How are you doing today?' Andrews and his cocky attitude. He had the audacity to reach out his hand for my father to shake. My dad did not take his hand. My father showed up for this meeting with a no bullshit attitude. He grabbed him by the neck, and then by his shirt in one swift move. He took him by his left arm and there he goes. It looked like Andrews was floating in the air. My dad had him lifted off of his feet and slammed him up against the wall. With his other free arm, he balled up his fist. My father's arm was cocked back in position ready to aim in direction. You could see it in his eyes when he changed his mind. He looked up at Andrews and said quite spitefully, 'You're not even worth it.' Now it's Andrews turn for his own lecture. My father would not hit the man, but he would question him. He would scream at him, 'How dare you hit my boy like that! What the hell is going on!?' He was furious. 'What is going on that these young kids deserve to be beaten up so badly for running away??' That is when I checked out, in awe of my dad. He's, he's sticking up for me. He is telling them how it isn't right. I just could not believe it. There were points of my dad yelling at Andrews that I could not even understand. All I remembered was it had something to do with running away, being out of bounds, and being away from the school. After my dad felt like he exhausted his voice with Andrews he made sure he was going to be able to check in with my siblings as well. So, we went and sat in the hallway outside of the auditorium. This is how we would visit, always in the hallway. We would get that visit with my brothers and my sister. After the visit was over my dad left my brothers and sister, but he took me along with him.

I remember going down the road. We were driving away from that prison. I wanted to cheer. I wanted to celebrate. I was free. My dad was taking me away from a place that had broken me into a million different pieces, in a million different ways. I felt guilty crossing that bridge. Guilty only because my siblings were not with us on our ride out. I knew what I was leaving, and how my siblings were still trapped in a mad house. Focusing on myself was all I could do. I could not help them; I was forced to focus on myself. I was not worried where I was going anymore because we were driving away from all that commotion. My next chapter started that day. The day my dad helped set me free.

By the time I had my time in court, my father had already passed away a few decades prior. He missed the justice that was able to be served to this despicable human being, Plint. I have strong traditional beliefs this court sentence is not Plint's final atonement. He will have more judgment handed to him once he leaves this world for all the atrocities he afflicted on me, and all the countless others.

CHAPTER *Eight*

I carried those words through some tough times later on

Finding a balance that works for you during your healing journey is important. You need people in your corner willing to call you out on your shit. You need people willing to listen to understand. You need a nonjudgmental area where you can vent and get it out. Having had counseling and had the best counselor, Carissa, I highly recommend it.

You are allowed to be angry, hurt, frustrated, nervous, and even scared. Healing and acknowledging your emotions are important. Remind yourself that you are a human being. You deserve to get to the other side of the hard stuff. You deserve to wake up happy. Healing through talking and getting through it is ugly, but you need to know there is a place beyond the hurt.

A phrase I grew up hearing through my father's healing was, it isn't our stuff to carry. All that hurt and mistrust, that was for the ones who abused them. They had their own karma to deal with. As survivors, you deserve to unload your shame in the act that was brought upon you, not asked for.

Intergenerational trauma and survival is our normal as a First Nation's person of North America. What our parents and grandparents went through in these institutions trickled through their own teachings one way or another. Each generation has a choice to make, to break cycles, or simply survive.

I caught you in my scope

My first job outside of the Alberni Indian Residential school was slashing bushes for a survey crew. My father got me the job, and it was nice and easy work. I was excited I landed this job. I was out in the forest being paid to slash bushes. I was out in the solitude of the forest doing my own thing. It was very freeing. I have been forced to endure all of this child labour that I was not being compensated for, so the idea that I was getting paid to cut bushes was fun. It was a nice easy job for a young boy. I thought, boy this is pretty easy. It was nice making my own money.

When I got home from the school, I made friends with Paul Tate and Reggie Joseph. We were buddies, and by summertime we seemed to be together a lot. We worked together slashing bushes. Having a job and being out of the school gave us that sense of maturity, feeling old enough to have a job and make money.

After being gone from the school for some time, I started feeling quite vindictive. I used to talk with my friends about this situation up at this school. We would talk about how abusive the institution we were trapped in. We were being abused and tormented for years, and it was nice to talk about it with people that understood. It was nice finally feeling some type of sympathy from what I had been living through for so long.

It does not take too long before you have all these ideas that naturally start swirling in your head. I have been gone longer then two weeks now, and the longer I spent away the more I start beginning to think about some type of pay back. I remember these ideas in my mind.

The survey crew we were working for had us stationed at a job in Lake Cowichan, and before we knew it were barreling down the highway. We were buckled up in my 1951 Ford, and I had a shot gun in the back. Vengeance was on my mind, and we had left work early for our little road trip. Before we knew it my Ford had been making the glide down the hump entering Port Alberni Valley. All of these triggers start coming up when we drive down river road; like they happened so many times before.

We drove down River Road, made it across the bridge to the Tseshaht reserve and swung a hard left after the bridge. We made our way to the school, and we just sat outside staring at it for a minute. This prison they called a school. These buildings and grounds held so much grief for me and being there brought something out of me. I began to climb a tree with my gun in tow. My gun was matched with a scope, and I started looking around.

There I was perched in this tree stalking these men that made me suffer. There he is, I found Andrews, he was in my sights. Nah, I thought, he was too easy. Andrews was the principal and finding him did not seem to be much of a challenge. My scope found its way to Plint. I found him. Reggie and Paul were down below from me, and they interrupted my thoughts with their concern. 'Come on bro, you can't do that. You kill somebody you're going to get into a lot of serious trouble.' It was a matter of fact, and they were not wrong. I listened to them and reluctantly lowered my gun. I began unloading it and lowered the gun down to my friends with a rope. They grabbed it from me, and we loaded up in my Ford and left. As we were driving away, you could almost see the trucks lights twinkling. A dance of excitement, almost as if to congratulate me in choosing my own peace over their violence. They do not get to define where I go. Those men do not get the gratification of locking me in another cell.

I had found myself caught up in a notion of redemption. It did not take me long to realize that it was not something I could ever live out. I understood playing out a situation like that would never be easy. Making a move, like killing my former abusers, would land me in jail. It was the 1950s in Port Alberni, BC, Canada. I was native, and my assailants were white men, there is no way I would not be hauled off to jail. Even if I had been the only one pulling the trigger, I am sure we would all be in trouble. Thinking back to those moments of that evening, it spoke to the integrity we held. We had the strength to walk away, and I would imagine not many could if they were handed the same chance.

'...You've got anger, you've got rage, that's understandable'

I was about 14 or 15 when I started working at the logging camp. When I was in camp the macho thing to do back then was to sit down with the boys and have a beer and play some poker. It is what the guys would do after a long day, or week of work. I will always remember what it was like when I first got to camp. I remember signing my papers of employment and leaving the office. The fellow that hired me had me pack my stuff and he took me to the bunk houses to show me which room I would be assigned to.

The room I was assigned to wasn't very big, maybe twelve feet by twelve feet. It housed two bunks and a cupboard. I threw my stuff on the bed and left the room. The lay out of the room reminded me of a supervisor room, so I felt the need to get out of there. The guy helping me find my footing asked me if I wanted anything to eat and I welcomed the idea of food. This place was not like the institution I had been used to. The camp had a big kitchen where I could help myself. He told me that there would usually be something left on the table for us to enjoy, but to help myself. What a nice change, I thought. This coming from the kid that would eat potatoes from the garbage incinerators and hopping the fence for fruits.

Reggie and Paul were employed with me at this camp, but they were assigned a different bunk to stay in. We were not put together and all these triggers start rising up. It always seemed weird at the time, like even in employment we were segregated. We were broken up and put into different areas. That day Reggie, Paul and I had spent more of the day down at the wharf. We were goofing off like most kids would and we started getting ready for the following day of work because it was a Sunday. Our first day of work was tomorrow. So, we spent the day kicked back and had our feet in the water in the local lake. When it started getting dark after supper, we would all find our way back to our bunks.

The room I was assigned to had another occupant when I got back to bed that night. I was horrified to find that there was an old white guy in the room when I returned. I thought, what the hell is this? What's going on here? My mind begins racing, and my tapes are playing. Here is this old white man, and we are in close proximity to each other. All I keep thinking about is abuse. My triggers begin to bombard my mind and my prejudices start kicking in. I started swearing at him, using profanities, and this would go on for some time. While I was working for this camp, I jumped right back into my survival modes. I began showering early in the morning to avoid being in the showers with other men. I would do anything to hide my body in hopes that no one would make an attempt in raping me. Those concerns do not just leave you because you have physically left the compounds of the school.

Finally, one day my bunk mate sat down and says to me, 'you gotta sit down and you gotta talk to me.' My bunk mate was one of those seasoned loggers that would cart around a case of beer with him and store it under his bed. My life had become trigger happy, and I would be triggered by so many different little things that would begin to overwhelm me. He was an old white man, who had a case of beer pushed under his bed, that he would drink daily. A bottle of beer at least on a daily basis. He would have one, or two beers and I'm sitting there getting anxious and stressed out wondering what's going to happen. My body is responding to his actions because it has been taught that harm will soon happen with conflict.

He looks over again and saying, 'You have to sit down son.' I looked at him and said, 'I am not your fucking son. Don't ever call me your son. Don't even think that I'm your son. I am not your son.' My anger did not stop this man from pushing more. He wasn't being negatively aggressive towards me, like I was used to. He still persisted, 'sit down, I want to talk to you. What's going on with your life? Why do you hate me so much?' This old white man is asking me about my life, about my triggers and why I was swearing at him. He wanted to understand me, and that was a first for me. I never had a white person want to get to know me after I meet them with aggression. I started talking in a more general sense.

'I hate white people. I hate them with a passion. I hate even being here in the room with you.' General honesty is what I went for. Something that was to the point so he would not misunderstand anything. He looks at me and says, 'what the hell happened in your life? What happened in your life that makes you so angry?' The pauses that soak through the room are so thick you can cut them with a knife. 'You are so angry, and even angry with me. Why are you so angry with me? I'm here because I've got a job. I have things to do, and I can't be in a room with someone that's angry with me' he says to me. He wants a resolution, and this is another first for me. He reaches out again and says, "You have to talk to me and tell me about this. We have to see if we can come to some kind of conclusion to this."

It dawned on me that I know exactly why I hate this man, but it does not have anything to do with him personally why I hate him. It was not supposed to be personal; I hated all white people at the time. So, I told him, 'You know something, I know the reason that I'm so angry. I just left a situation.' I found myself stumbling to find the words, but the words come to me. It is like a bandaid I have to rip off. Here we go I thought, 'I was in a boarding school, and I was physically abused, and I was sexually abused.' A gust of understanding filled the room. This old white man and I were sitting across from each other trying to find a way to make our living situation work. I was sitting in front of a man that cared enough to ask, and that was different for me.

'Ohhhhhh. Okay. Well, you have prejudice.' You can tell this man is trying to find the proper words to use to get his point across. 'That's understandable. You've got anger, you've got rage, that's understandable.' He goes on and eventually says to me, 'you're entitled to be angry, but the way you deal with anger, is that you can't direct it at me. I haven't done anything to you. You and I, we gotta be getting along together. We're bunking in the same room together. If we have to remain this way, then we have to start getting along because I can't stand the fact that you're in here and you're mad at me. You're angry with me, and I haven't done anything to you.' What he said was making sense. Maybe I did show up with a preconceived notion that he would hurt me. Maybe I did get anxious when he'd drink, I mean, he was bigger than me. The one thing I did know for a fact before we sat down, was I hated him because he was white.

He looked over at me and said, 'You have to understand one thing, and that one thing is that all white men are not the same. You have to quit generalizing.' This also makes a bit of sense. Most of the white people that I had to interact with abused me to an extent, so it was hard to break that habit of generalization. I was still a kid when I was working out all of these big emotions. He broke my thought and concluded his message with, 'I have a wife, I have children. I have the loveingest family that I could ever imagine to have. I feel very fortunate as a human being. At my age, I still love my family.'

That was the start of my recovery. I will always remember that moment. I always remembered his words. I carried those words through some tough times later on. We got along after that talk. We would become best of buddies. Even though he was this old, white man, we got along. That moment was a moment where you look back on your life and realize that significant change happened in those moments. That man changed my life.

CHAPTER *Nine*

I know that a lot of people
really don't understand how
therapeutic this is for me.

*The very moment where relief set in, and a breath could be taken.
They had won their case against Plint. This photo was taken after
Judge Hogarth's final address in 1995.*

I was six when my Dad started his first journey into these court cases. So, most of my life has been surrounded by conversations about the Alberni Indian Residential School. Conversations surrounding any experience within AIRS use to be hush, hush. It was a group of men who took Arthur Henry Plint to court. It was men who recounted their memories of countless abuses by this man. In 1995, a group of men won their court case against Plint. He was put away for crimes of abuse. 9 months after we lost my dad to cancer, a letter came in the mail. It would have been my Dad's 55th birthday, and we received word that Plint had died in jail.

Before these court cases were concluded, the Residential Schools of Canada were not considered a form of genocide. My father, and the students of these institutions were determined to change that narrative within Canadian history.

The following words were his exact words he spoke when he was made to give his final address to court in 1995.

Final words in Provincial Court in 1995

March 21, 1995

The court has asked for a final statement in his court proceedings vs Arthur Henry Plint, proceedings were adjourned, and the judge was to make his decision.

I want Your Honour to understand, and the court to understand, that we see no remorse in this man. He inflicted pain on us as children. We can't wash away all of that stuff, all of the hurts.

You, Arthur Henry Plint, sentenced me to an eternity of Hell. You sentenced me to a life without a childhood. You took that away from me. You cannot give that back to me. You took away the pride of my people. Any length of time in jail will never ever bring that back.

You see all of these people here, with the blessings of all our women, are rebuilding our lives. But we have to go through this in order to try and alleviate the problems that you caused.

The sexual atrocities that you committed on us are absolutely unforgivable. On me, especially is unforgivable, but I was told that I should forgive you. I find it really difficult to do that. Because you forgive people, our people have known this understanding, that we forgive people that are remorseful.

You show no remorse to us. You have not apologized to me for the things that you have done to me. You have not apologized to my people for all of the injustices that you inflicted on us. To me, that adds to a lifetime sentence. To me, that adds to my shame that you caused me.

I am always thankful that we have had respectful elders and grandmothers. My grandmother ceremoniously rid me of a lot of the shame that you instilled on me. Respectful elders in our community. They done things to us that this system of counselling and this system of justice cannot do. They re-instilled a pride in who we are, and that is our own help, your honour. That's our own help. I love that help, because without that, a lot of us would have been in situations further with suicidal attempts, much like my brothers and myself have been in. We would have been able to inflict ourselves with a great deal of drugs and alcohol abuse; the shame that this man put on me.

I want you to know that I climbed out of that. I climbed out of all those substance abuses through the help of my elders, my family, my people. The pain this man inflicted on me, there is no sentence this court can do that will do any justice, but I appreciate you listening to us and me. Kleco Kleco.

Within the first draft of my Dad's victim impact statement for the 1995 court case, he also had an extended version that included the following words:

"I have transferred the internal pain into external anger and aimed it at my family, my children, my wife, and others, all of them feeling the fear of this learned behaviour of mine.

So, Arthur Henry Plint, you did not only violate me, you were partly responsible for the abuse of my family and others at my hands with what I learned, while in your care as a child care worker for nine years. You were charged with my supervision as a child because of the then Federal law, which was inflicted on me as a Native Person, demanding my presence at the Alberni Indian Residential School.

You, Arthur Henry Plint, taught me those parenting skills which fostered physical and mental abuse. Violence was the order of the day. You, Arthur Henry Plint, taught me to use alcohol during my nine year stay at Alberni Indian Residential School, to ply sexual favours from me. Including, oral copulation, rectal penetration, stroking, fondling, unwanted kisses, as well as unwanted butt stroking.

Also to inform me, it was okay to escape the dreaded realities of our young lives by using alcohol to numb the pain.

I charge you with the theft of my childhood, Arthur Henry Plint. You stole from me the chance of being my own child as well as the child to my mother and father.

It was you, Arthur Henry Plint, who made me set aside my emotions and finally stifle them, to grow up and not be trouble by your aggressions. I was troubled by everything you did to me, and I remain troubled to this day.

I want you to imagine, Arthur Henry Plint, the overpowering fear you instilled in me as a child at the possible loss of my parents, adding further to my traumatic experience of actually being there at the Alberni Indian Residential School.

I charge you, Arthur Henry Plint, with the responsibility of accepting the monstrous pain I received as a child from you, as our caregiver at the Alberni Indian Residential School."

Final words in Supreme Court in 1999

Four years after a group of men took Arthur Henry Plint to court, and won, my father decided he would take matters farther. For my father, he wanted his story on record. He wanted to make sure his memories were put in black ink and sealed within the Canadian legal system to its highest standard. He wanted to be sure that people understood what those institutions created, what they stood for, and what they taught. Those employees were monsters raising children. Some of those being dishonourably discharged men and women from the Canadian armed forces.

I am so incredibly proud of my father and his strength to come forward and say, "This is what they did to me." My dad was changing the world around him. His court cases led to monumental change to many First Nations people across Canada. He is, arguably, one of the many reasons why we were led towards the 'Truth and Reconciliation' we see today.

The following words were his exact words he spoke when he was made to give his final address in court in 1999.

August 17, 1999

The supreme court has asked for a final statement in his court proceedings vs Arthur Henry Plint, the Government of Canada, and the United Church of Canada, before proceedings were adjourned, and the judge was to make his decision.

I am very thankful of processes like this, irregardless of how hard it is *(sic)*. To be given an opportunity to be talking about these kinds of things, I know that a lot of people really don't understand how therapeutic this is for me. Its like purging everything, purging, purging, purging, getting rid of it. All of this excess baggage that I packed around for my entire life, it wasn't mine.

You know, as victims, as a victim, you know, I want to erase this notion of being very nostalgic and how I carried my life on; all of the 'I wishes' that didn't happen. You know, I wish I wasn't born. I wish I was born white. I wish that I had different parents. I wish there wasn't a guy by the name of Plint. I wish that Andrew survived so that he could be here in front of me. That nostalgic notion doesn't carry me through my life, and I've learnt that. Those kinds of issues, I've learned to accept the fact that I do have a history, and that history has made me who I am today. I believe this human being, a contributing human being to society, one that has contributed artistically both to the state at large and to my own community at large. I've contributed, I feel, enormously to this society with my artist background. And it hasn't come without consequences, and those consequences are having to relive the notion that I represent all of my assailants. And I understand that in my heart that's a very sickly thing to pack around. So, purge that, let it go. Public at large is a lot better than, you know, the assailants that are named in this suit.

It has never been about the state. It has never been about the church. It's been about the assailants. Because my remembrances of the state and I, in the later part of my life, is that we have done lots of good work together. We have represented this country well. I don't have any workings with the church. My only recollection of the church is that we had a very nice man live in our village. His name was William Wickerbee. A very consoling man, an understanding human being. I remember confiding in him about some of these issues and the understandings that he had. He would wrap his arms around me. I admired that man, and he was the United Church minister. I remember going into his church, in Clo-oose with my mother. I never wanted to go to church because of my connection. My mother took me there, most of the time against my wishes. I wanted to be doing fun things and my recognition of that building was not a pleasant one. But I knew that man that worked inside, that was doing work for our people, very compassionate human being. He did lots of good for our Indian people. I know that. His name comes up and I have nothing but good to say about him. That my remembrances

The Defiant

of church. So, it's never been about the state or the church, it's been about the assailants and what they have done to me. How they changed this little boy into this violent human being. But with the strength of all the people, most of them that sit in here. They seen a better human being inside, and they helped with that recovery.

I'm extremely proud of my people because they seen something in me that was special. I've contributed back to my people artistically. I've given back to our communities, things, objects, objects of pride, head dresses. Those things that instil pride back in our people. I'm proud to say that I've done things like that.

I really thank you, Your Honour and all of you that sit here, you know for giving me this opportunity to say this, to tell my story. It means a lot to me. The fact that all of these things happened. The fact that all of these things followed me all throughout my life, has really been troubling to me because what I needed to do as a human being was to let these things go. Let go and leave them there, get rid of this baggage, get rid of all of these tragic events that I packed around all of my life. Hurtful things that go on, that came from these institutions. They weren't mine; they weren't my people's; they were hurtful, and I really want to thank you for this opportunity to talk about this.

It means a great deal to me. It means a great deal to my people that these stories come out. They're tragic stories. They need to be told because what that does for them, it helps create an understanding amongst everybody. It's not just me, it's everybody that's in the public at large that needs to understand that these institutions actually were in place, they happened, they're a part of our past. I accept my past; I have to in order to go on. If I don't accept it, then I can't grow as a human being. And in growing it makes me a better human being and I contribute greater to society. That's what I want. That's what I've always wanted in spite of my troubled past. There's a lot of good accomplishments there and we all, as Canadian people benefit from that. Wherever

I travel, we all benefit from it. Irregardless of what you think of me, I still represent you, artistically. And I am proud of that because I have a proud people here. And I represent a proud race of human beings. And I have to say, proud survivors too, because we have struggled, we have struggled for, in some cases five generations of this, and we pack around all of these fears, all of this anger, all of the anxieties that we come with, that we pack around with us on a daily basis. It's not ours. I know this.

I really thank you for giving me this opportunity. It hasn't been pleasant. It's been a real struggle for me and I'm sure that will continue to be a struggle. Even though this opportunity was given to me through my attorneys, it'll continue to be a struggle for a long time because I have lots of issues to deal with, with my family, my people and that's hurtful. Thank you, Your Honour.

Conclusion of first draft of Victim Impact statement

In summary, I want to say that there are four, and in some cases, five generations of my people were abused and acculturated in this fashion. The many abuses that were inflicted and painfully received often led to death caused by alcohol, drugs or suicide. This was the only way for some to escape the pain caused by that inhumane educational system staffed by people like Arthur Henry Plint. Those of us who survived that institution are truly survivors in the greatest sense.

I will make sure to tell my story to my children. They are the ultimate victims, because of my acting out my learnt behaviour of reprehensible people like Arthur Henry Plint.

The most demoralizing, spiritual abuse that the institution ever inflicted on me was turning my own people on me because of my light colour hair and fair skin tone. I was handed statements like, 'You sure are a whitey, must have been a good white man around your momma'. This to me was the most unforgivable situations.

Many of us have sought traditional means of healing. We have also received counselling services outside our village systems. For me, breaking the silence inflicted by Plint and the countless others, and reliving the torment has subjected me and my family to ride on an emotional roller coaster. Silence was fearfully implanted in me by Plint's intimidating, humiliating, terrorizing, and shame-based abuses. The hell and shame I lived while under Plint's supervision, have slipped away but the echo of my memories never will. Now, ultimately, I want justice to be served. Nazi war criminals met their final demise in answering to the world for their atrocities. Plint, as more of our people become willing to reveal their accounts of your assaults against them, you should be held accountable for your behaviour.

A Daughter's Epilogue

Before Port Alberni's walk for our first recognized National day for Truth and Reconciliation (September 30, 2021), I was approached to write a piece about my father and his experiences at Alberni Indian Residential School. This was the first time I ever sat down and read my fathers testimony from both of his court cases. After having read all of the legal documents my family was able to keep from all of those years ago, I knew I'd be writing this manuscript. For the first walk of Truth and Reconciliation I wrote a three page write up on my father's experiences that my brother/cousin/uncle Ken Watts read out loud for me in front of a number of residential school survivors, their family members, community members, and allies/supporters. The strength it took to read those raw words out loud, was enormous. My father meant a great deal to Ken, and vice versa. For Ken to have read that for me in my absence meant the world. I was that proud little sister watching via Facebook live. Weeks after that piece was read out loud, I was still receiving "Thanks" for my having shared my fathers experience because it helped changed perspectives. I created an impact that I had yet to understand. Our people were finally able to have a bit of understanding of the residential schools and the experiences that the former students may have witnessed, or experienced, because not all survivors spoke about their experiences of this institution. The reaction from my having written that piece solidified my choice to write this book.

During November 2021, I took time from each day to write my father's experiences from the Alberni Indian residential school. I completed 28 different chapters within the month of November. It was addicting to me. I felt as if I were completing a mission I was meant for. There were days I would find my cheeks drenched in my own tears, reading and re writing my fathers words within his court testimony. My dad's story became so impactful in court because he had the help of my Mom, a student in criminology, to create a powerful story. My mother was learning how the power of your words in your written statements made incredible impacts. As hard as it was on my mother, she would encourage my father to be as descriptive as possible when it came to his testimony in court. She would ask him the hard questions, like how the abuse would make him feel in those moments, both emotionally and physically.

After writing this memoir, I became depressed. These memories were so big, that I should have made sure I released my emotions better. I thought because I would do my best to disconnect from the story being my father's that I would be okay. Writing this story was not easy, but I knew it was the right thing to do and it was the right time. This journey has taken me 2 years and 3 months to complete before I hand it over to my publishers. After all this time, I truly believe everything came together the way it was meant to at the right time.

The amount of conversation surrounding the residential schools the past two years, has been extremely triggering for me to navigate. My entire childhood and adolescence was encompassed by healing from my parent's association with the residential schools. You could say that I, myself, have been healing from the aftermath of the residential school system my entire life. After I lost my father in 2003 to cancer and I was only 3 months into being 15. I was quite young to have lost my father. There were a few adjustments I had to make after he was gone. There were important people in my life that left, and honestly, I don't really know why they did. As an adult I justify those actions of their absence to grief, but the little girl version of me still stands there crying from the abandonment. Some people came back and explained why they left, and we were able to rekindle a relationship lost. With the lost of some important people in my life, and the loss of my father, the conversations surrounding the Residential School's were put on hold. There wasn't much of a reason for my mother and I to chat about it, and back then it was just us.

When Tk'emlúps te Secwépemc (Kamloop's First Nation) searched for the remains of those 215 children, it changed my world. It was a blunt reminder of where I came from, and who my father was. My father was a loud advocate for residential school survivors. He was willing to share his experiences to navigate conversations of understanding. He needed his story heard because he wanted the world to know that no matter how hard this system tried to break him, he found a way to be whole. My father found peace with his experiences and wanted to help others find their own sense of peace as well. As a survivor of abuse, he deserved to feel validated and heard. He used his voice to shed light on what came after. When these children entered the doors of these institutions they never walked out with the same innocence. These children grew up hard. They were raised in institutions that essentially staffed pedophiles, and well groomed adults in understanding their role in colonizing these children to a white washed standard. These children would have their identities stripped and given numbers to neutralize them.

I am my father's youngest child. Being the baby sister of my siblings has been a treat. I didn't grow up with all of my siblings, nor did we always keep in touch. Life tends to run busy for all 10 of us. One thing I have always known for certain, being the baby of my siblings meant that I had the healthiest relationship with our father. By the time I came along, my two oldest siblings already had 4 children between them, so, as you can imagine there is a ten year age gap with about half my siblings. Each of us had a completely different and unique relationship with our father. He impacted our lives and I know he is with each of us still to this day. He was always a family man; he just didn't always have the healthiest tools to extend his beliefs to all of us equally through our time with him.

A common misconception about the Canadian residential school system was that the events that conspired on their institution grounds did not affect anyone living today. I was never registered to a residential school as a child, but my father went to one. My husband was never registered to a residential school, but both his paternal grandparents were enrolled in one. These institutions caged generations of children in a system that was meant to destroy their character and eliminate their culture. When our country took those generations of children, they took away chances of the ability to pass on our traditions in healthy settings. The abuse the children endured in these institutions changed the way they would carry themselves throughout their lives and it would change the way their future children and grandchildren would be raised. These institutions raised dysfunctional adults and released them back into the world where they were ashamed of an upbringing that was forced upon them. Silence and shame would be some of the main reasons why many survivors would not talk about their experiences. Bottling up their emotions would lead to unhealthy ways of coping with their trauma. For most, these unhealthy coping mechanisms would lead to repeating negative cycles of repeated dysfunction intertwined throughout many parts of their lives. Some of these children would one day turn to alcoholism, drug use, suicide, or further abusive cycles to numb whatever pain they were pushing down. This would lead to passing on those dysfunctional cycles onto their children.

In walks the stereotypical Canadian native, but honestly, what does that even mean anymore? For myself, I remember growing up in the 90's with the knowledge of understanding that natives were stereotyped to be alcoholics, unkept, and if they owned their own home, it would be located on a reserve, most likely also unkept and probably filled with children. With the many generations of beautiful human beings starting each day with the goal to crush these stereotypes, we are slowly starting to gain traction on moving away from this typical stereotype. Those beautiful people refused to feed into an unbroken cycle that was not serving us positively. Breaking cycles is not easy but has proven to be worth it.

Our younger generations have started asking questions, and the power that knowledge has brought forward has been profound. We are living in a time where race abuse is no longer being tolerated.

People are being called out on their blunt use of stereotypes and discrimination. The power of technology has given people the power to show discrimination struggles, as well as powerful moments of fellowship. During current events, we have towns, cities, nations, and even countries that now show support in race topics, such as the police brutality against George Floyd and the 215 children's remains found in the grounds of a former Canadian residential school. People are no longer willing to remain silent over race injustice. I do personally still encounter the few people that are still unwilling to change their minds on social injustice, but the many that will listen to understand outweigh the few by a lot. This is exactly why the current conversations surrounding the former Canadian residential school systems are so overpowering because people are ready to be open to conversations about these histories.

On February 21st, 2023, Tseshaht First Nation held a conference to share their first round of findings with ground penetrating technology surrounding the Alberni Indian Residential School. They shared with the world that through their in-office research they can prove that 67 students did not go back home after entering this institution. Through their ground penetrating technology, they have discovered 17 potential unmarked graves. The saddest part of this news was that this is only a mere 12% of the covered area they are going to be researching. There will be more children to follow. There were more then 70+ different registered Nations of children that were sent to the Alberni Indian Residential school. The registered Nations effected stretched across Vancouver Island and reached across the water to the mainland of British Columbia, extending all along the West Coast. The year 2023 marks the 50th anniversary of the Alberni Indian Residential school closing its doors for the final time.

This book was written to give my father a voice again. This is his story, and it is so heartbreaking to know that it is just one story. A story of one boy in this broken system of thousands of Indigenous children. A story of a boy who was broken, but escaped and survived the many traumas that he packed around for decades. A story about how our people were treated in an unjust society where the primary goal was to take away all of those special things that made us First Nations of Canada.

I am working on putting together the next half of his life following this book. While his story in these institutions were so important to share, so is his story of healing. The person he was when he left that institution, was not the same man I said goodbye to in 2003. My father was the strongest man I knew. He was and still is an inspiration to many. He touched many hearts and helped for many causes throughout his life. He accomplished so much in his 54 years on this earth, and I am excited to share those triumphs too.

To end, I would like to share the final paragraph in my Orange Shirt Day piece that gave me the push to write this book in 2021. This piece was shared by being read out loud on the former institution grounds of the Alberni Indian Residential School on the first recognized National Truth and Reconciliation Day in Canada.

Dad, they are listening. Your voice is still being used after all these years. Your story is still being heard after we laid you to rest in 2003. Thank you for paving a long, hard, road for our people. Thank you for starting the hard conversations. Education is key. Understand that we as a people are going to run into conflict about these traumas. Understand that if these survivors could not talk to their own family, their spouses, their children, about the traumas endured at these institutions, that we also can not expect our outward world to understand our trauma right away, but we can educate them on it. It is time for our people to heal and end those cycles of hurt that were so freely given to us in those institutions. That hurt passed down in many different forms from our Grandparents, or Parents. Living generations of survivors are still here today, in every nation you can encounter. The world is starting to open their eyes on the situation, and its going to be a long road. My father won his court case against one of his main abusers in 1995, 29 years ago and still to this day, people are just starting to learn about those histories. Do not stop. Do not stop educating people. Do not stop healing. Do not stop growing from these traumas. We deserve to stand tall and be proud of who we are, and what we come from. That is the gift I was able to receive from my father, he raised me to be proud of who I was, who I come from, and where I come from. I will never stop giving my father a voice of his experience.

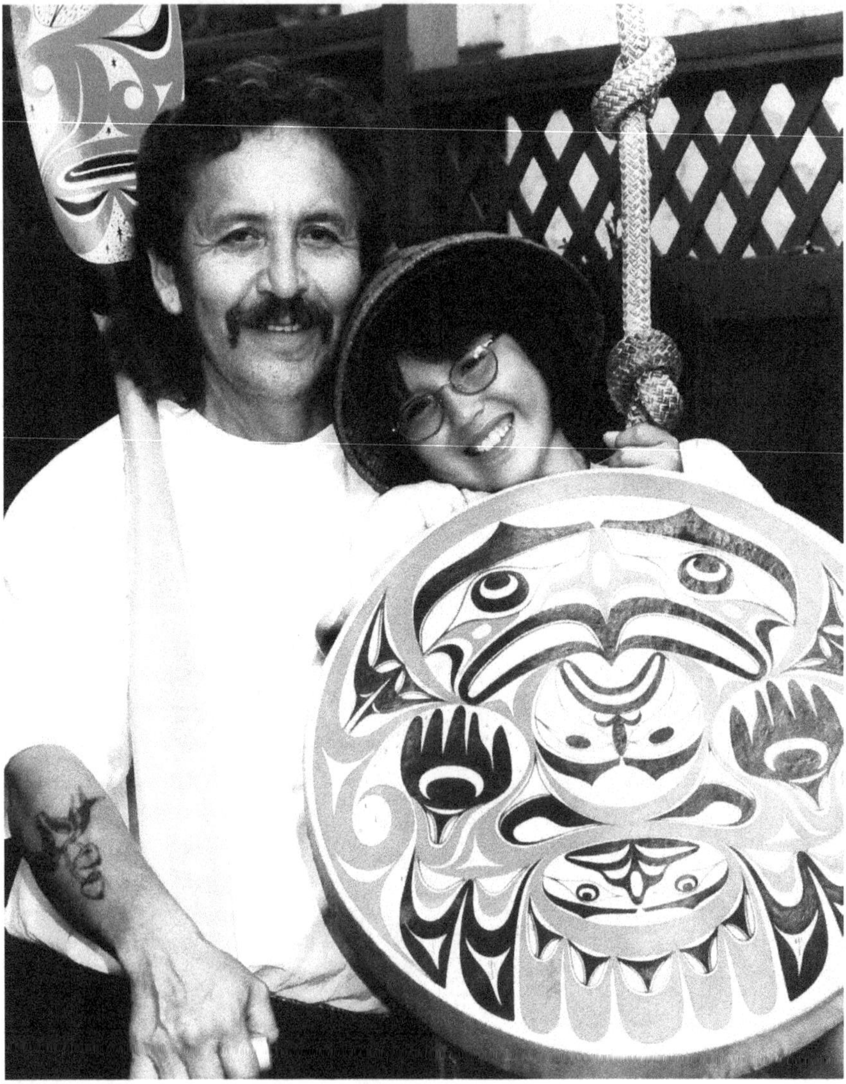

About the Authors

Evelyn Thompson-George promised that she would never let her father's voice disappear. In an era where such conversations were rare, **Art Thompson** bravely recounted his experiences at the residential school, encouraging more Indigenous Survivors to come forward and talk about their experiences.

Art worked tirelessly throughout his life to ensure that his family, Canada, and the rest of the world knew and understood what happened to him and many other Indigenous children and families. Her father was also a great teacher for Evelyn, and she has carried on his legacy by writing his memoir and sharing his story with future generations so that they too can learn and heal.

Evelyn won second place in a Victoria School District writing contest for First Nations students. Her essay, entitled "My Inspiration" and written about her father, was published in Duck Soup for the Aboriginal Soul. Evelyn now lives on the traditional lands of the Tsleil-Waututh Nation (North Vancouver, BC), with her husband, Ernie, and children, Ivan, Ernie Jr, Benjamin, and Vivian.

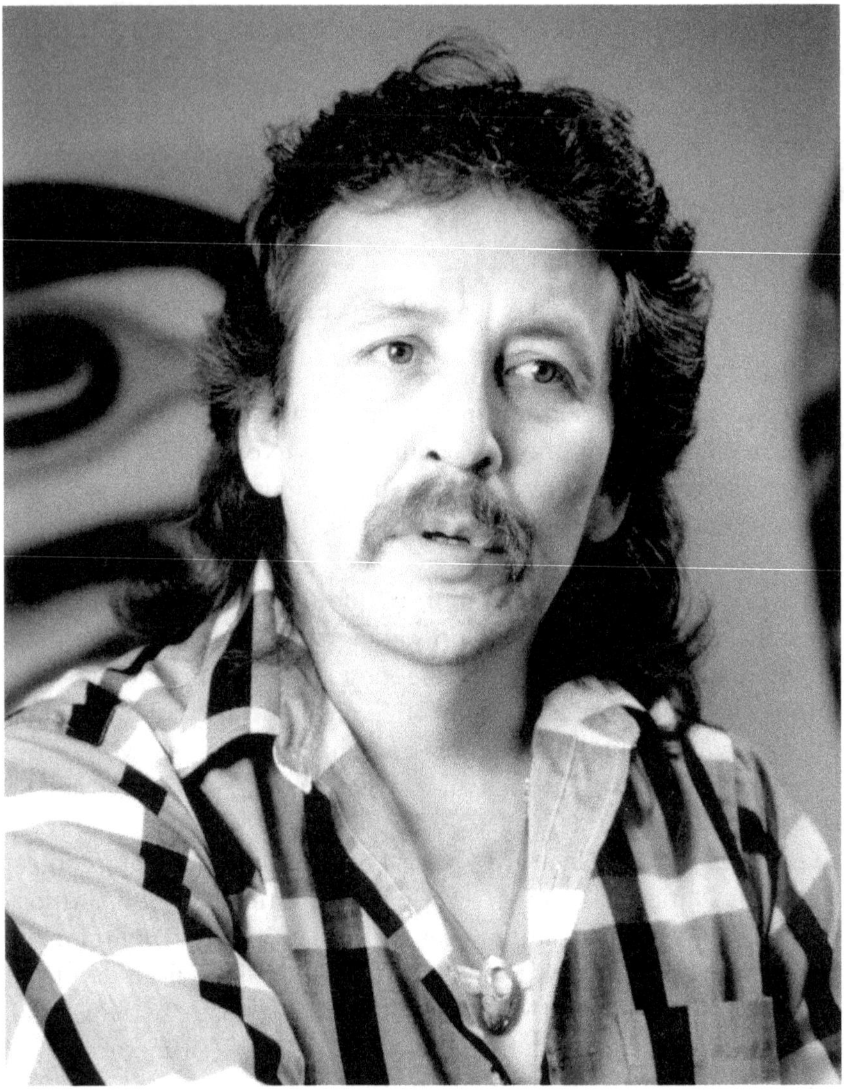

For the people who knew **Art Thompson**, we knew him to be a Master Artist, a World renown Nuu-Chah-Nulth, more specifically Ditidaht, Contemporary Artist, a Residential School Survivor and Advocate, a Philanthropist, a Civic Leader and a Mentor.

Art Thompson's Grandmother, Helen Mary Thompson encouraged him to pursue the arts. She would tell him that he would contribute to his people with the gifts he was given with his hands. When he was a baby, his Great Grandfather, Tooqbeek, rubbed medicine on his hands; to give him that ability to be good with his hands. His grandmother would reinforce those Teachings and remind him of his gifts. He would go on to share stories of his people's legends and histories through his art.

Art Thompson studied Art at Camosun College in Victoria where he focused on painting and drawing. These courses helped bring his art to life. Later enrolling into Emily Carr in Vancouver. This is where he was introduced to Silk Screen Printing, significantly impacting a void in the art world of Nuu-Chah-Nulth and Northwest Coast art.

Art Thompson's contributions include, the design of the 1995 Queens Baton and medals presented for the Commonwealth Games, recipient of the Citizens Award from the city of Victoria, the design of the 1997 Indigenous Games logo, the award recipient for the Indigenous Awards for Arts and Culture in 2000. These would be his most public accomplishments.

At the end of his career, Art Thompson was an internationally recognized Nuu-Chah-Nulth Artist name. He made an assortment of art, notably, Totem Poles, Masks, Transformation masks, Bentwood boxes, Paddles, Gold and Silver engraved jewelry, Curtains for Ceremony, Head dresses, Shawls, Oil paintings, Silk Screen printed prints, to name a few. He enjoyed experimenting with new mediums and bringing new ideas to life.

www.ingramcontent.com/pod-product-compliance
Lightning Source LLC
LaVergne TN
LVHW020434190325
806321LV00002B/221